SMALL-SCALE TEXTILES

DYEING
AND
PRINTING

T0272872

SMALL-SCALE TEXTILES

DYEING AND PRINTING

A handbook

John Foulds

Intermediate Technology Publications 1990

Published by ITDG Publishing
The Schumacher Centre for Technology and Development
Bourton Hall, Bourton-on-Dunsmore, Rugby, Warwickshire CV23 9QZ, UK
www.itdgpublishing.org.uk

First published in 1990
Print on demand since 2004

ISBN 1 85339 028 3

A catalogue record for this book is available from the British Library

ITDG Publishing is the publishing arm of the Intermediate Technology Development Group.
Our mission is to build the skills and capacity of people in developing countries through the dissemination
of information in all forms, enabling them to improve the quality of their lives and that of future generations.

Printed in Great Britain by Lightning Source, Milton Keynes

CONTENTS

ACKNOWLEDGEMENTS

Even a small handbook such as this cannot be compiled without the help of many people.There is no room to mention them all, but I would particularly like to thank staff, students, and ex-students of the Textile Department at West Surrey College of Art and Design, Farnham, Surrey; Tristram Bartlett, ITDG Project Officer; and the Tropical Development Research Institute for permission to publish illustrations from *Dyeing of Sisal and other plant fibres* by A. J. Canning and C. G. Jarman (1983).

John Foulds

Illustrations and diagrams by A1 Studios Limited, Leamington Spa, and Mike Calvert, Rugby.

FOREWORD

This handbook is one of a series dealing with small-scale textile production, from raw materials to finished products.Each handbook sets out to give some of the options available to existing or potential producers, where their aims could be to create employment or sustain existing textile production with the aim of generating income for the rural poor in developing countries.Needless to say, this slim volume does not pretend to be comprehensive.It is intended as an introduction to the topic which will stimulate further enquiry.Although each handbook is complete in itself and provides useful reference material on each specific area of production, the series, taken as a whole, does reveal the breadth of technology required to equip a small-scale textile industry.While being primarily technical, the series also covers the socio-economic, managerial, and marketing issues relevant to textile production in the rural areas of developing countries.

The author of this handbook has harnessed his own particular expertise and experience to produce a distillation of his technical knowledge applied to the developing world. While no single package of technology can be appropriate to all situations, he has produced a simple but logical progression covering all aspects of small-scale textile production. Production of this series of books has been sponsored by the Intermediate Technology Development Group (ITDG), as part of its efforts to help co-ordinate the most appropriate solution to particular development needs. This series forms part of the cycle of identifying the need, recognizing the problems, and developing strategies to alleviate the crisis of un- and under-employment in the Third World.

ITDG also offers consultancy and technical enquiry services. For further information write to ITDG. We will be pleased to help.

Martin Hardingham,
Textiles Programme Manager,
ITDG, Rugby, UK

PREFACE

The art of colouring textiles is very old. Its history can be traced for at least 4,000 years, starting in India and gradually spreading through Persia to Phoenicia and Egypt. All colouring materials used at that time were naturally occurring products, the roots, stems, leaves and fruits of plants and the dried extracts of certain insects and shellfish. It is interesting that indigo, originally from India, and the famous Tyrian purple, were both vat dyes, derivatives of which are still manufactured and used today.

The fibres being dyed at that time were also natural products, wool and hair fibres, cotton and linen. In many cases, particularly cotton or linen, the dyes used could only be successfully applied with the aid of a mordant, which was usually an inorganic salt of iron, copper, or tin, which was able to combine with the dye and improve its take-up by the fibre.

Later, during the Renaissance in Europe, the art of dyeing became a skilled occupation and its secrets and methods were jealously guarded by dyers' guilds. There was little fundamental change in this situation until the middle of the nineteenth century, when the discovery of colouring matters derived from coal tar products began; and from that time there has been a relatively rapid development in the manufacture of a wide range of dyes for both natural and man-made fibres. At the present time about 6,000 dyes for all fibres are made by hundreds of companies throughout the world and hardly anything is manufactured which does not employ the products of the dyestuffs industry.

Modern dyes fall into groups, each of which is applied most successfully to a particular group of fibres and, to a large extent, an understanding of the chemical structure of fibres and the nature of the dyeing process has enabled dyeing and printing to become a knowledge-based industrial process, rather than an art relying on a considerable degree of skill.

This is one reason why the use of dyes derived from natural products has not been included in this handbook: their use requires a considerable degree of experience to obtain reliable and consistent results. In general, natural dyes must be considered and used as individual products often with their own idiosyncratic properties and methods of application. None form groups, such as acid, direct, or reactive dyes, with similar dyeing properties and a complete range of colours. Colour matching by dye mixing is not therefore possible and since most dyeing and printing will be undertaken to meet a specification of some kind, even if only for a particular colour with particular fastness properties, it is essential to have a range of dyes available to meet these specifications. The colour fastness of many natural dyes, at least of those which have been tested, can also be inadequate to meet many specifications.

This handbook is therefore concerned with the principles and practices of dyeing and printing, based on the use of modern chemical technology, but applied to small-scale textile production with all its particular problems. It is perhaps fortunate that dyeing and printing can be carried out without the use of complex or expensive equipment: indeed, some of the latest techniques are most successful when used in a labour-intensive way on a small scale.

1. INTRODUCTION TO DYEING AND PRINTING

This handbook is limited to the consideration of dyeing and printing on a small scale — processes which can be carried out by hand or by the use of small power-driven equipment. It is also assumed that, as dyeing and printing are essentially service activities, they will form part of a larger activity of making textiles, probably as part of a small commercial operation. Considerations of cost, reproducibility, and the need to meet normal commercial demands for fastness properties will therefore be important considerations. The handbook will also be limited mainly to the dyeing and printing of wool, silk, and cotton, since a large range of other fibres, particularly synthetic fibres such as polyester, often require the use of expensive equipment and therefore fall outside its scope.

General considerations

Dyeing and printing as a way of enhancing the appearance of textiles has been used for a long time. Very little fundamental change took place in methods until the discovery of synthetic dyes in about 1856. Since that time there has been a proliferation of dyes designed to meet an ever-growing demand for textile products which are both attractive and practical. All dyes, whether from natural sources or manufactured, are coloured organic chemical substances which have the ability to be taken up and retained by fibres, normally from a solution of the dye in water. Because of the great number of different fibres and other materials which need to be dyed or coloured in some way, and the extremely wide variation in the kinds of wear and tear they must withstand in use, there are many thousands of different dyes. All must however possess certain basic properties if they are to be effective as dyes:

(a) Intense colour
(b) Solubility in water, either permanently or only during the dyeing operation.
(c) Ability to be absorbed and retained by fibres or to be chemically combined with them.
(d) Fastness — the ability to withstand removal or destruction by the processes which the fibre undergoes in manufacturing or in normal use.

(Source: Giles, C.H., *Laboratory Course in Dyeing,* p.29. Society of Dyers and Colourists.)

Modern dyes give the most satisfactory combination of these properties for any desired end use. Moreover, dyes are normally designed with specific fibres or groups of fibres in mind, and are usually grouped according to the type of fibre for which they are most suitable.

All fibres have a similar internal structure, in that they are composed of molecules which are extremely long and thin, like the fibres themselves. The way in which the molecules are arranged largely determines a fibre's physical properties, such as strength or elasticity, and some of the chemical properties, such as the ability to take up water or dyes. Sometimes the molecules are packed together lengthwise very closely and sometimes they are arranged in a more random manner. Where they are closely packed the fibre will be strong and rather rigid, and water and other substances cannot penetrate the fibre structure easily. Where they are more randomly arranged the fibre will tend to be weaker but elastic, and will readily take up water and other substances. All this, of course, is on the most minute scale, but the result is that fibres have a very large internal surface, composed of the walls and channels between molecules, and it is on these internal surfaces that dyes and other chemicals are taken up.

Fibre	Main dye groups used for dyeing
Wool and hair fibres	Acid, metal complex
Silk	Acid, metal complex, direct, reactive
Cotton, flax, jute, viscose rayon	Direct, vat, azoic, sulphur, reactive
Acetate rayon	Disperse
Nylon	Acid, metal complex, disperse
Acrylics	Basic, disperse
Polyesters	Disperse

(This list is not meant to be comprehensive. The same groups would be used for printing, with one or two additions. Coloured pigments have not been included. They are used mostly in printing, when they can be applied to most fibres by bonding to the surface.)

When a fibre is placed in water, the water rapidly penetrates and swells the fibre structure by entering through minute pores in the surface. Dyes and other chemicals are then able to diffuse into the spaces between the molecules and there combine with the fibre or form some other kind of link with the fibre or other dye molecules.

Although it is not normally possible to tell in a simple manner how the molecules are arranged in a fibre, a rough indication is given by the amount of water the fibre will normally hold in a moist atmosphere. This is called moisture regain (MR).

FIBRE	WOOL	VISCOSE	SILK	COTTON	ACETATE	NYLON	ACRYLICS	POLYESTER	POLY-PROPYLENE
MR %	16	12—13	11	9—11	6	3.6	1—2	0.4	0

Illustration 1 Moisture regain of fibres

Fibres with a very low MR are in general rather difficult to dye, mostly because their internal molecular arrangement does not allow water or dyes to penetrate very easily under normal conditions.

Once a dye has penetrated the structure of a fibre, various chemical forces come into play so that the dye is gradually taken up and retained. The rate at which this takes place is determined by many factors. If the dye is taken up by the fibre very quickly from the dyebath the material being dyed may not be uniformly coloured. If the dye is taken up by the fibre too slowly, it will result in increased fuel and labour costs. In the first case an even dyeing, one in which every part of the fibre and the material being dyed is uniformly coloured, is difficult. In the second case the cost of dyeing becomes too high because of the increased fuel and labour costs, and the fibre may be damaged because of the prolonged dyeing time.

In practice, therefore, the dyer must use various means to control the rate of dyeing, usually by varying the temperature of dyeing and by adding various chemicals to the dyebath. Raising the temperature apparently increases the rate at which the dye is taken up, and this is used in many dyeing methods to allow dyeing to take place in a reasonable time. It cannot be done too quickly or there will be a risk of uneven dyeing. The dyebath is therefore gradually heated (raised) to the final dyeing temperature, normally 80 to 100°C, and complete dyeing will take about one hour at that temperature. In the case of fibres with a very compact physical structure, such as polyester, the best way to obtain a reasonable dyeing time is to raise the temperature to about 130°C, which means that very expensive pressurized dyeing machines must be used.

It is important to note that because dyeing takes place on the internal surfaces of fibres, time must be allowed for the dye to penetrate the fibre structure, and so most dyeing methods are designed to allow this to take place in about one hour. If a fibre is cut across into very thin slices during dyeing and these are examined under a microscope, it will be seen that the dye gradually penetrates from the outside to the inside of the fibre. If dyeing is stopped with only the outer layers of the fibre dyed (ring dyeing), it would have poor colour value (weak colour) and fastness properties.

The addition of various chemicals to the dyebath is also used to control the way in which the dye is taken up by fibres and can thus also influence the evenness of the dyeing. The use of these will be described in detail when the dyeing of individual fibre groups is discussed in Chapter 2.

CHOICE OF DYE

Choosing the best dye for a particular dyeing method, which will give all the required fastness properties required in the final product, requires considerable knowledge and experience. Quite often, of course, the choice may be limited by considerations of cost, availability, customer requirements, or simply by colour. Where considerable choice is possible, the following factors should be considered when choosing a dye for a particular purpose:

(1) The form in which the material is dyed

If fibres are dyed in the loose state, the evenness of the dyeing is not so important since blending of the fibre mass takes place during yarn manufacture and so any unevenness of colour will tend to be lost. This may mean that faster dyes can be used which might have uneven dyeing properties: faster dyes may indeed be essential, since loose fibres must withstand much processing during manufacture into fabric. If fibres are dyed in yarn or fabric form, however, evenness of dyeing is important since the slightest unevenness will show in the finished fabric. If the dyeing method does not allow a very good circulation of the dye solution or movement of the material being dyed, which is often the case when dyeing by hand, it may be necessary to use dyes with very even dyeing properties or to modify dyeing methods to allow for this.

Illustration 2 Dyeing cotton yarn by hand in Bangladesh

(2) The manufacturing process
Many parts of the manufacturing process after dyeing may influence the choice of dye. Woven cotton fabrics must generally be scoured in hot alkaline solutions and any dye used must withstand the process. Fabrics containing wool must often undergo severe wet treatments such as scouring and milling, and the dyes used must withstand these processes.

(3) The fastness properties required in use
More often than not these are dictated today by customer specifications, and dyes and methods must be chosen to meet these. However, where precise specifications are not available it is sensible to choose dyes with very good light fastness for articles which must withstand severe exposure to sunlight, or good wet fastness for those which must be washed frequently.

These are only a few of the considerations underlying the choice of a particular dye for a particular purpose. There are obviously many more and often a compromise must be reached between the colour which may be desired and that which is achievable to meet all the fastness requirements on a particular fibre.

Colour matching

This is the ability to reproduce any desired colour on the material being dyed. There are really two requirements when dyeing any colour: first, that the dyeing shall be carried out properly so that it is even and has good fastness; second, that it should be the desired colour. The first is relatively straightforward, the second requires experience and skill to carry out consistently.

The desired colour will usually be available, from a customer or from records, as a sample of dyed material. This should be of the same type as that being dyed: it is nearly impossible to match yarn to a coloured piece of pottery, for example. The most reliable way to reproduce the desired colour is of course to have a 'recipe' from a previous dyeing of that colour on that material. Failing this the dyer must rely upon his previous records of dyeing similar colours. It is most important that the dyer understands the basic principles involved in colour matching, so that any colour can be reproduced to order, rather than relying entirely upon recipes, and so that dyeings which are not the correct colour can be changed easily. Colour matching is obviously a large and important subject, since one of the most important requirements for dyeing in a commercial situation, even on a very small scale, is that the dyeing or print is the desired colour. These matters are discussed in more detail in Chapter 2.

Printing

Printing can be regarded in many ways as localized dyeing. Thus the same dyes would be used to print various fibres as to dye them: the fastness properties of the dye are the same dyed or printed, and colour matching is just as important in printing as in dyeing. Printing however can use many techniques not available to the dyer, and the printer must use different methods to 'fix' the dyes, which is the equivalent of carrying out the dyeing process successfully. Printing is much more concerned with technique and method than dyeing and these are described in detail in the appropriate Appendices.

The basic methods of printing fabrics are however straightforward and have been used for many years.

Making designs directly on the fabric

This is probably the oldest method of patterning a fabric using dyes or pigments, but of course the person making the pattern must be skilled in drawing. The simplest method is to paint directly on the fabric and there are many techniques which allow dyes and pigments to be used in this way. Once the dye or pigment has been applied the fabric must be given a suitable treatment to allow the dye to be properly taken up or the pigment to be fixed.

The first methods of working directly on the fabric probably relied upon painting the pattern on the fabric with a substance which formed a physical barrier to the dye: when the fabric was then dyed these areas resisted the dye to form the pattern ('resist printing'). This method was used before dyes existed which gave good fixation simply by direct hand-painting. A wide variety of substances can be used as a resist for dyes, from those which form a simple barrier such as starches, gums, clay, wax, or methods of sewing or tying the fabric tightly in patterns, to the use of resist pastes which contain mordants or chemical resists.

The essential feature of all these methods is that the 'designer', by working directly on the fabric, produces a unique article which cannot be repeated exactly. The methods are therefore most suited to the production of relatively small articles, but the capital outlay needed can be very low.

Making designs directly and transferring them to the fabric

This involves a wide variety of techniques, all of which take the original 'design', such as a painting or a photograph, which can be converted into a form which can be transferred to a fabric. If the original design contains many colours each of these must be separated out, since almost all printing processes apply colours to fabric separately, and all the colours must of course 'fit' together when they are applied to the fabric and so reproduce the original design. There are three ways the design can be converted into a form suitable for printing on fabric:

(a) by making each colour in the design into a raised surface, on a block of wood or metal. The raised surface is used to pick up dye or pigment to transfer to the fabric, and each block must 'fit' so that the design is reproduced exactly;

Illustration 3 Block printing fabrics in India

(b) by making each colour in the design into a pattern cut below a flat metal surface. The dye is applied to the whole surface, then the excess is scraped off the flat area to leave dye only in the part cut below the surface, which can then be transferred to the fabric. Again, each colour must fit;

(c) by making each colour in the design into a pattern cut through a metal or paper sheet or formed on a fine mesh or screen. The dye is pushed through the holes in the stencil or screen on to the fabric. Each stencil or screen must again fit.

The essential features of all these methods is the separation of the production of the original design from the method used to transfer it to fabric. This means that the design can be repeated exactly as many times as needed, and the methods are therefore suited to the production of many identical articles or to printing long lengths of fabric. The capital cost can vary from moderate to very high depending on the degree of mechanization which is introduced.

6

Transferring designs directly to fabrics using a high degree of mechanization

The latest developments allow the production of multicolour designs on computer screen which can then be transferred to fabrics directly by means of electronically controlled printing systems. The essential features of these methods are extreme flexibility and speed of operation which makes them suitable for a wide variety of printed effects, but the capital cost is extremely high.

All the methods described, with the exception of painting by hand, have been developed in a number of ways for different purposes. Block printing has been mechanized by mounting the blocks on rollers:one version uses blocks made from plastic foam to print carpets. Screen-printing has been developed in similar ways using rotary screens. In every case, as the degree of mechanization and speed of operation increases the capital costs rise and the latest printing systems are extremely complex and expensive. For these reasons the only printing methods which will be considered in this handbook are those which can be carried out simply by hand, that is, direct hand-painting, hand block-printing, and hand screen-printing.

No matter which method of printing is used it is essential that there is good collaboration between those who originate the designs to be printed and those who carry out the printing.

2. BASIC PRINCIPLES AND PROCESSES

Dyeing wool and hair fibres

This is a large group of fibres all having the same general characteristics in that they are grown by a wide range of animals as a protective fleece which is removed by shearing, or some other method, either at short or long intervals of growth. They are all similar from the dyeing point of view in that they are all protein fibres with a similar chemical structure, but are extremely variable in other respects. Each fleece, even from one animal, may have a wide variety of fibre types, from fine fibres in the underfleece to long coarse guard hairs. Fibres from some animals will be coloured to a greater or lesser extent and all will contain grease and sweat salts produced by the animal during growth. Three processes which take place before dyeing are therefore extremely important:

1 sorting the fibres into groups based upon some property e.g. colour;
2 scouring, that is removing the grease and sweat salts;
3 blending the sorted and scoured fibres to give as uniform a mixture as possible. (This may take place after dyeing.)

Each of these processes is very important from the point of view of good dyeing. Having a mixture of different coloured fibres will obviously make dyeing difficult, but fibres of different thickness will appear different depths of shade even when they contain the same amount of dye. Fibres in the fleece also suffer varying degrees of exposure to weather, sun, etc. during growth, which usually means that the tips of the fibres are slightly more weathered than the roots. This can also bring about a variation in dye uptake along the length of each fibre.

Any gross unevenness in the final blending before spinning will therefore inevitably mean that dyeing appears to be uneven. This unevenness must not be confused with a yarn which has been made from an even blend of fibres, which of course will always contain fibres of different thicknesses and degrees of exposure. These will always dye slightly unevenly, but these differences give dyed wool its unique appearance and 'sparkle'.

Since scouring and blending wool are generally most effective when undertaken on fairly large-scale machinery, small-scale processing without such aids usually means uneven treatment which can then cause dyeing problems. This may or may not be very important, depending on the type of product for which the wool is intended. If the wool is to be hand-spun with drop spindles followed by hand-weaving a degree of unevenness in the final product may be acceptable, but this aspect should always be considered carefully when planning small-scale production of wool textiles.

Wool and hair fibres have a high moisture regain, as mentioned in Chapter 1. This is an advantage for dyeing, since the fibre easily takes up water and therefore dyes, but it does mean that the fibre can also take up other chemical substances with which it comes into contact and is thus easily damaged, in particular by alkalis or bleaches containing chlorine. Even 'normal' yarn dyeing can bring about a strength loss of about 20%. The fibre is also unique in possessing a surface scale structure, giving it the frictional characteristics which cause it to 'felt', that is, to become entangled with other fibres into a permanent mass. This is brought about by movement in hot and wet conditions such as a dyebath. Care is therefore necessary when dyeing to handle the wool gently without too much agitation, or loose wool will be difficult to open, blend and spin, yarn may become felted and unuseable, and fabrics may become too compact and form permanent creases. It is possible to treat the wool to minimize the possibility of felting, but this process is probably outside the scope of small-scale processing and if it is carried out badly it can damage the wool severely.

Preparation of the wool before dyeing

Loose wool and hair fibres should always be scoured before being dyed. Yarn and fabric will probably contain some oil, added to aid spinning, and dirt picked up during processing. They should be scoured by the methods described in Appendix 2. Clean, scoured loose wool, yarn, and fabric can be stored in clean cold water overnight before dyeing, but if they are to be stored any longer they should be dried after scouring.

Choice of dyes

The dye groups available for wool and hair fibres are acid and metal complex. It is possible to use other groups or individual dyes, but these sometimes require special methods. Acid dyes are probably the most important and widely available — all major dye manufacturers offer a range — and they can be divided into three sub-groups with different properties of levelling (evenness of colour) and fastness. Each group has a complete colour range.

Dye group	Dyeing conditions	Properties
Equalizing acid dyes	Strongly acid (sulphuric acid) (pH 2-3)	Good levelling Poor wet fastness
Milling acid dyes	Weakly acid (acetic acid) (pH 4-5)	Moderate levelling Good wet fastness
Super milling dyes	Almost neutral (ammonium acetate) (pH 6-7)	Poor levelling Very good wet fastness

The light fastness of dyes within each group can vary from high to low, and so the dyes must be carefully selected for a particular end use. It is obviously not a good idea to mix dyes from different sub-groups since they require such different dyeing conditions. All are easy to apply by the methods described in Appendix 3 or by following instructions in the manufacturer's pattern card, if this is available.

Examples of some manufacturers' trade names:

Equalizing acid dyes Lissamine (ICI), Supramin (Bayer), Erio (CGY)

Milling acid dyes Coomassie (ICI), Supranol (Bayer), various (CGY)

Super milling dyes Carbolan (ICI), Alizarin (Bayer), Polar (CGY)

(All dye manufacturers offer the same dyes, or near equivalents. If you cannot obtain a particular dye from one manufacturer, it is more than likely that another will be able to offer the same dye under its own trade name.)

Metal complex dyes are those which are able to form a 'complex', that is, a combination of dye plus a metal ion of some kind, which together have better properties than the dye alone. Sometimes the metal, in the form of a metallic salt, is applied to the fibre separately as a mordant — for this reason this group are sometimes called mordant dyes. The most common used is chromium so the term chrome dye is also used. There are really two sub-groups, chrome dyes and pre-metallized dyes in which the metal is combined with the dye during manufacture. The most important type of pre-metallized dyes are those in which 2 dye molecules are combined with 1 metal atom, known as 2:1 pre-metallized dyes.

Chrome dyes are applied to wool in the same manner as milling acid dyes and are then 'aftertreated', that is, given a separate treatment with a solution of a chromium salt (usually sodium dichromate). The colour of the dye can be quite different from that of the metal complex, which can make colour matching tricky. The group is characterized by having very good fastness to wet treatments although in general the colours are dull, which is usual with dye/metal complexes.

The 2:1 pre-metallized dyes are applied to wool in a similar manner to super milling dyes and of course do not require any aftertreatment. They possess extremely good wet and light fastness but again the colours tend to be relatively dull.

Dye group	Dyeing conditions	Properties
Chrome dyes	Weakly acidic (acetic acid) (pH 4-5)	Medium levelling Very good wet fastness
2:1 pre-metallized dyes	Almost neutral (ammonium acetate) (pH 6-7)	Poor levelling Very good wet fastness

The light fastness of chrome dyes can vary from moderate to very good, while in general the light fastness of 2:1 pre-metallized dyes is excellent. The dyeing methods for both groups are described in Appendix 3.

Examples of manufacturers' trade names:

Chrome dyes Diamond (Bayer), Eriochrome (CGY), Salicine chrome (HOE)
2:1 Pre-metallized Isolan (Bayer), Irgalan (CGY), Remalan fast (HOE)

The choice of dye for a particular purpose is very difficult, as mentioned in Chapter 1, and depends upon many factors. If loose wool is being dyed it is important to choose dyes which will withstand all the subsequent processing, particularly all the wet treatments. In this case it would be almost essential to use pre-metallized or chrome dyes. Wool yarn and fabrics must be as evenly dyed as possible, and dyes must be used which have this property, without sacrificing other properties such as washing fastness which may be needed.

Cost is always a problem and in general the cheapest combination of dyes should be used which will give the required shade and fastness properties.

DYEING SILK

Silk, like wool, is a protein fibre but its chemical composition, though similar, gives the fibre slightly different dyeing properties. It is grown by the silkworm and extruded as a fine filament which forms the larva's cocoon. Each extruded filament is in fact two silk fibres held together by silk gum (sericin) produced by the worm. An important treatment before dyeing or printing is therefore to separate the fibres from the gum, known as degumming or boiling off. This is achieved by a prolonged scouring process, which must however be gentle enough not to damage the fine filaments in any way. Once silk has been completely degummed, its characteristic lustre and softness is achieved. As in the preparation of all fibres, it is important from the point of view of even dyeing that the degumming is carried out as evenly as possible.

Preparation of silk before dyeing

There are many variations in the methods used and in the extent of degumming to produce silk for a variety of purposes, but in general three different types of product are available.

(1) Ecru silk (bast silk), from which only 2 to 5% of the gum is removed and the scouring process is used to merely remove dirt and some silk wax.

(2) Half-boiled silk (matt or souple silk), from which 8-12% of the gum is removed.

(3) Boiled-off silk (cuite or lustre silk), which is completely degummed.

Each variation will be used for a different purpose: ecru silk is often used in the warps of fabrics so that the gum protects the fibres during weaving, while other types are softer and more lustrous and will be used as weft etc. The filaments can vary in colour from almost white to pale brown, much of the colour being in the gum, and some of the wild silk from uncultivated worms (tussah) can be quite brown in colour. A proportion will also be processed as silk waste, produced during reeling from the cocoons, and this is spun into yarn in a similar manner to wool and cotton.

In a short handbook such as this it is impossible to cover all the treatments which silk might undergo before dyeing or printing. The processes described in Appendix 2 are therefore intended to be used for the complete degumming of the fibre.

Choice of dyes

Silk, like wool, has a high moisture regain and therefore takes up dyes easily and can be coloured with a wide range of dyes.

The dye groups most commonly used to dye silk are acid, metal complex, and reactive, and sometimes direct dyes may be used for a particular colour. Generally only milling, super milling, or 2:1 pre-metallized dyes will be used and the dyeing methods will be similar to those used for the same dyes on wool with some variations described in Appendix 6. Reactive dyes for cotton can also be used to dye silk and can give very bright colours with very good fastness properties. The fastness properties of acid and pre-metallized dyes will be similar to the same dyes when applied to wool. Basic dyes were at one time used to give very bright colours but in general they have very poor fastness properties.

DYEING COTTON

About half of all the fibre processed in the world is cotton. It is therefore the most important of a large group of fibres, all having similar dyeing characteristics in that they are composed of cellulose which forms part of the seed, stem, or leaves of plants. The group also includes flax, ramie, hemp, and jute. There is also a range of fibres manufactured, or regenerated, from materials containing cellulose such as wood pulp or waste cotton. The most important of these regenerated cellulosic fibres is viscose rayon.

Since these fibres are grown in a wide variety of conditions throughout the world they can have different properties depending on their origin and therefore sorting, mixing, and blending is an important aspect of processing before manufacture into yarns. Unlike wool or hair fibres, cotton is rarely scoured in the loose state but usually in the form of yarn or fabric. Most of the other cellulosic fibres need some kind of fibre separation and purification process before spinning.

Preparation of cotton before dyeing or printing

Since cotton is not normally scoured before being spun, a scouring treatment is essential before yarn or fabric can be dyed or printed successfully. Scouring is carried out to remove waxes and mineral matter and to make the material absorbent and ready to dye. Bleaching may also be necessary for white fabrics or where the material is to be dyed a pale colour, since the natural colour of cotton can vary from pale cream to light brown. Good, even preparation is therefore an essential first step before dyeing and the methods described in Appendix 2 should be regarded as the basic minimum necessary.

Choice of dyes

The dye groups available for cotton are direct, reactive, vat, azoic, and sulphur. Again, it is possible to dye cotton with other groups but these often require special equipment or methods.

Direct dyes are the simplest group. All major manufacturers offer a range and they are applied to cotton and other cellulosic fibres simply by heating the material in a solution of the dye, with the addition of common salt or Glauber's salt to increase dye take-up. They are divided into three sub-groups which require slightly different application conditions.

Dye group	Dyeing conditions	Properties
Class A	No special precautions.	Good levelling properties. Poor wet fastness.
Class B	Salt must be added slowly during dyeing.	Moderate levelling properties. Moderate wet fastness.
Class C	Salt must be added slowly during dyeing; careful temperature control is needed.	Poor levelling properties. Moderate wet fastness.

As a group they have only poor to moderate fastness to wet treatments, although a number of aftertreatments can be used to bring about some improvement. These are too numerous to describe here but one method is included in Appendix 2(h). Some of the aftertreatments can reduce the light fastness appreciably and change the colour slightly.

The light fastness can vary from poor to very good and this is generally how they are grouped for sale, although different classes can be found in every group.

Examples of manufacturers' trade names:

Moderate light fastness Chlorazol (ICI), Diphenyl (CGY), Benzo (Bayer)

High light fastness Durazol (ICI), Chlorantine fast (CGY), Sirius supra (Bayer)

Reactive dyes for cotton are now a very important group and are widely available from most manufacturers. They are applied to cotton and other cellulosic fibres in a similar manner to direct dyes, but once taken up by the fibre can be made to react with the cellulose in a manner which chemically links the dye to the fibre. When properly applied they thus have very good wet fastness properties and are of special interest since one type can be applied from a cold dyebath, with a potential saving in energy costs. The same type can also be used in printing to bring about dye fixation without the necessity of steaming the fabric after printing. There are now a very large number of types available but they are generally grouped according to how reactive they are. Others may be made especially for printing etc.

Dye group	Dyeing conditions	Stability of the dyebath
Highly reactive	Dyeing temp. 30°C. Reaction brought about by sodium carbonate	Moderate
Moderately reactive	Dyeing temp. 85-90°C. Reaction brought about by sodium carbonate and sodium hydroxide	Good

Reactive dyes as a group give bright colours which are fast to washing on cotton, linen, etc.; the light fastness can vary from moderate to good. All are easy to use by the methods described in Appendix 5, although some care must be used when applying the highly reactive types in order to obtain an even dyeing. In all cases it is very important to remove the dye which has not reacted chemically with the fibre by a hot washing process if good wet fastness is to be achieved. In some cases, particularly if dark colours have been dyed or printed and the yarn or fabric is going to be stored for any length of time in humid conditions, the material can be aftertreated as described in Appendix 2(h).

Examples of manufacturers' trade names:

Highly reactive dyes Procion MX (ICI), Levafix E-A (Bayer)

Moderately reactive Procion H-E (ICI), Cibacron E (CGY)

Vat dyes are one of the oldest groups for cotton. Indigo and Tyrian purple are naturally occurring vat dyes. The dyes are insoluble in water but can be converted to a water-soluble form by reduction with sodium hydrosulphite and dissolving in caustic soda. This process is called 'vatting' and the temporarily soluble dye can be applied to cotton then returned to its original insoluble form by oxidizing in air or with an oxidizing agent.

After dyeing the material must be boiled in soap solution to develop the true fastness properties and colour. As a group vat dyes are relatively difficult to apply, requiring considerable skill to obtain an even dyeing with simple equipment, but they have outstanding fastness properties. The group contains the fastest of all dyes.

Examples of some manufacturers' trade names:

Caledon, Durindone (ICI), Cibanone (CGY), Indanthren (BASF)

Because of the extremely valuable fastness properties many developments have taken place in this dye group, mostly to make application easier. Many water-soluble ranges are now available, but they remain very expensive both to buy and use.

Sulphur dyes are applied in a similar manner to vat dyes, but are vatted with sodium sulphide. They are a cheap dye to buy and use but with a restricted colour range. They are used mostly to dye wash-fast blacks, browns, and navy blues on cotton fabrics.

Azoic dyes, or insoluble azo dyes, are formed in the fibre by chemical reaction between two substances, a 'coupling' component and a 'diazo' component. The material to be dyed is first impregnated with the coupling component dissolved in caustic soda, squeezed to remove excess and then immersed in the diazo component, when the coloured dye forms inside the fibre. By choosing different diazo components it is possible to obtain a range of colours from one coupling component, but the colours possible are mostly red, orange, or yellow with only a few dull blue colours. These dyes are relatively cheap to buy and use but again require some care in application, particularly to ensure that the dye does not deposit on the outside of the fibre giving very poor rubbing fastness. Like the vat dyes, they must be boiled in soap solution after dyeing to develop their true colour and fastness properties. Many developments have taken place with these dyes also, in particular the manufacture of stabilized mixtures of the two components which can be made to join on steaming, making them very suitable for printing.

Examples of some manufacturers' trade names:

Coupling components Tulathols (Atul)
Diazo components Tulabase (Atul)
Stabilized mixtures Rapidogen (Bayer)

NOTES ON DYEING TECHNIQUE

The various dyeing methods described in the Appendices are all based upon the use of a standard method for a particular dye group. The quantity of dye, the dyeing assistants, and the amount of liquid in the dyebath are all based upon the weight of the material being dyed, so it is important to know this weight accurately. Thus a method which recommends the addition of 10% Glauber's salt to the dyebath means that if 4540 gm (10 lb) of material is being dyed, 10% of that weight, i.e. 454 gm, of Glauber's salt must be added.

Weight of reagent or dye needed =

$$\frac{\text{weight of material to be dyed} \times \% \text{ required}}{100}$$

$$= \frac{4540 \times 10}{100}$$

$$= 454 \text{ gm}$$

The volume of the dyebath is also determined by the weight of material being dyed. Thus, using the same example, if a method requires that there should be 20 times as much dyeliquor as the weight of material, the dyebath must contain 20 x 4540 = 90,800 gm or 90 litres approx. In practice the ratio of the weight of material to that of the dyeliquor (Liquor Ratio or LR), is determined largely by the size of the vat available and the ease with which the material can be handled in it, and quite often the same vat will be used to dye widely different weights of material. However, the LR is important particularly when making repeat matching dyeings, as any variation in LR between dyeings will mean a different amount of dye being taken up.

For this reason it is important to know the capacity of each dye vessel being used. Each should have its own dipstick which has been calibrated in, say, 5 litre steps. If the volume of dyeliquor is known it is then very easy to add reagents where the quantity is specified in grams/litre: for example, if 2 gm/litre of reagent is needed and the capacity of the dyebath is 90 litres, so 2 x 90 = 180 gms of reagent is needed.

The material being dyed should be moved in the dyeliquor during dyeing so that each part has even treatment. This movement should be increased immediately after the addition of dissolved dye or dyeing assistants. Indeed, where possible the material should be removed from the dyebath completely during these additions. Where this is not possible, as in dyeing some fabrics, it is often advantageous to add the dye or dyeing assistants more slowly than recommended in the methods if there is a danger of uneven dyeing. When dyeing wool yarn it is very important not to move the material about so much that yarn starts to felt.

The measurement of the acidity or alkalinity of the dyebath is important for some dyeing methods, such as when using acid dyes on wool. This is most easily done by the use of universal test papers (pH papers). The papers are available in most countries from chemical suppliers. If the dyer relies only on the quantities of reagents given in the dyeing methods, there is a danger that allowances cannot be made for what has happened in previous processes. For example, if yarn scouring left the yarn containing too much alkali some of the acid added for dyeing would be taken up in neutralizing this and the dyebath would then not contain enough acid. If test papers are not available the dyer must rely upon the quantities given in the methods and judge from the final result whether they are correct.

Quite often it is necessary to make small adjustments to the shade of the dyed material at the end of dyeing since the first dyeing was not quite 'on shade'. This process can be tricky and needs much experience to carry out consistently. The dyes to bring about the change must be added very carefully and the material must be moved vigorously in the dyebath during the addition to avoid uneven dyeing. The dyebath should also be adjusted before the dye addition so that the dye is not taken up too quickly, usually by reducing the temperature or the concentration of reagents by diluting the dyebath with water. Since a very small quantity of dye is being added, it is important that the fastness properties, especially to light, are at least as good as the dyes in the original dyeing.

Buying good quality materials is essential for consistent and accurate dyeing and printing. Most major dye manufacturers will at least maintain an office in most countries, even if they do not import directly, from which pattern cards and technical information about the company's products can usually be obtained. They will also usually supply information about how their products can be obtained, the addresses of principal importing agents, etc. It is important to deal only with a recognized agent of the manufacturer.

Basic principles of printing

Printing textiles, that is, producing a pattern of some kind with dyes or pigments, is almost as old as dyeing itself. A printed fabric may be produced by a very wide variety of methods, some simple and cheap to carry out, others requiring the use of very complex and expensive equipment. In this short handbook it will only be possible to give a very brief description of some of the more important aspects, particularly those of interest to the small-scale producer. For fuller details many excellent textbooks on the subject are recommended in Chapter 7.

In general, textile fabrics will be printed with the same dyes used for dyeing. There are of course specialized dye groups used only for printing, and most textiles can be printed with pigments bonded to the surface, but if printing is part of a small dyeing and printing operation there are obvious advantages in being able to stock the same dyes for both. In these circumstances printing can be considered to be localized dyeing and to achieve this it is necessary to prepare the dye in such a manner that:

1   A suitable printing paste is made up which contains most or all the dyeing assistants necessary for good dye take-up and fixation on the fabric. In addition, the paste must be thickened so that the dye is contained in the paste when it is applied to the fabric and during the time and under the conditions which are used to bring about fixation. This is usually achieved by making a paste which contains a thickening agent, which may be a natural gum or starch product.

2   The thickened printing paste must be just the right stiffness or viscosity to be printed so that it does not spread from the area to which it is applied, and it must then normally be dried on the fabric.

3   The printed fabric must then be given a treatment which allows the printing paste to act as a localized dyebath, so that the dye is transferred from the paste to the fabric without spreading into surrounding areas of fabric. This is normally achieved by steaming the fabric so that the hot and wet conditions allow dyeing to take place.

4   The fabric must then be washed to remove unfixed dye, thickening, and dyeing assistants without causing staining of unprinted areas.

Preparation of the fabric for printing

Fabrics must be prepared for printing at least as thoroughly as for dyeing, since in some cases dyeing conditions are far from ideal during printing: a good colour yield depends considerably on how thoroughly the fabric has been prepared. Cotton and linen fabrics should be given at least the scouring treatment described in Appendix 2. Wool fabrics are considered difficult to print, mostly because of the difficulty in preparing the fabrics so that good colour yields and evenness can be obtained. Some form of chlorination treatment is generally considered essential to achieve good printing on wool, but these processes require very careful control and are really outside the scope of a small printer. The printing method described in Appendix 7 does not require pre-chlorination and gives good colour yields on wool without steaming, but it requires careful technique to be successful. Silk fabrics must be thoroughly degummed before they can be printed successfully.

Even when a cotton fabric is being printed with pigments it is important that the fabric is well prepared: poor scouring will result in poor pigment fixation.

Locating the fabric during printing

The fabric must be located securely during the printing operation, even where it is a semi-finished item such as a tablecloth, a scarf, or even a garment. This helps with both the application of the printing paste and, in the case of a length of fabric, it ensures that the finished print is accurately placed and that all the colours fit correctly. Small items can be stretched lightly over frames or pinned to a slightly resilient flat surface. It is important to allow for the fact that some of the printing paste will 'strike through' the fabric on to the surface underneath, and this surface must be changed or washed between each print to avoid 'marking-off' on the back of the next print. If only one side of a garment is being printed it can be placed over a plastic or metal former which is the shape of the garment and printed and dried on the former, which can then be removed, washed, and reused.

The article being printed must not be distorted too much by fixing down, or the print will change shape when the fabric is washed and relaxed after printing.

Lengths of fabric which are block or screen printed must be fixed to a table of the type shown in Illustration 4. Again, it is important that the fabric is not distorted whilst it is being fixed to the table. This may be achieved by pinning to a 'back grey', a cotton cover fixed to the table which is removed and washed after printing, or by gumming directly to the table when it has a waterproof cover.

Preparation of the printing paste

A power-driven mixer or high speed stirrer is needed to make up most printing pastes successfully. It is possible to make up some pastes with a hand-operated mixer or even without a mixer, simply by hand-stirring, but this is generally slow and does not give a good mix. When making up emulsion thickenings of the type described in Appendix 9 a high-speed stirrer is essential. The mixer can be purpose-built or simply a propeller type driven by an electric motor. The mixer should have its own container for the paste being mixed which is suficiently large to avoid splashing. A good general rule when making up printing pastes is: always add thin to thick — in other words, always add liquids to thickeners etc.

The most suitable final consistency for the printing paste will vary, depending on the printing method being used. The recipes given in the Appendices will give a useful general consistency, but the quantities of thickening used should be varied as experience and conditions indicate. The most important aspect of any printing recipe is to maintain the correct proportions of reagents in the paste if changes are made (such as reducing the strength) in much the same way as maintaining the concentration of reagents in a dyebath.

Application of the print paste to the fabric

Once the paste has been made for a particular dye group to be applied to a particular fibre, there is a wide variety of methods for transferring it to the fabric being printed. The consistency or viscosity will have been adjusted to that which experience has shown gives the best results for the application method being used.

Where very simple methods of direct painting by hand are intended, the printer has great freedom of choice: brushing, painting, etc. — almost any method can be used. The aim must be to produce an even layer of paste on the fabric, as any unevenness such as thick or thin places will show on the finished print. Direct hand-printing also includes the painting of a wide variety of resists — gums, starches, resins, waxes (batik) — and also a number of ways of tying or sewing the fabric into patterns. In these forms of resist printing the fabric is dyed by a suitable method before removal of the resist. This process may be repeated many times to produce a wide variety of printed effects. In general these techniques can be undertaken with the minimum of equipment, and if the non-steaming methods described in Appendices 7 and 8 can be used, the capital outlay can be very low although with a very high labour content. The processes rely upon a high degree of skill in the printer to produce an attractive effect and much practice is necessary when starting these processes.

Printing with blocks needs a slightly higher capital outlay, a source of suitable blocks is needed and whilst the type of equipment shown in Illustration 4 is not absolutely necessary, printing is much easier with it. The printing blocks can vary widely: they can be made of hard plastic foam, cut in linoleum, etc., but are most often made from wood, either built up from several layers or carved from a solid block. One block is needed for each finished colour in the design, and where multicoloured designs are printed the blocks must be made with great skill so that the colours in the pattern 'fit' in the finished print. The wood used for the blocks must be stable and not shrink or warp during the frequent wetting and drying which takes place. The blocks must of necessity be fairly small for ease of handling. To some extent this has limited the types of pattern which can be printed, unless a very large number of blocks are used to make a large design — but this is usually not economic. It is also very difficult to apply an even layer of printing paste over large areas of fabric from a wooden surface, and so large plain areas of the block are usually recessed, leaving only a wooden outline, the recessed area being filled with a hard wool felt pad. Where multicolour blocks are used it is normal to fit 'pitch pins' on the blocks at well-defined points, so that accurate placing is possible during printing.

An even layer of printing paste is picked up on the block from a layer of blanket in the floating tray and then transferred to the fabric, the block being struck with the heel of the hand or a small mallet. Each colour in the design is applied in sequence, and the fabric is then either dried on the table or removed to dry by hanging.

Block-printing can be very versatile and, although the pattern area can be small, it is possible to fit a printed design to particular parts of a woven structure in the fabric being printed, which is impossible in screen printing. The type of equipment needed is shown in Illustration 4. Table construction is not critical but the top should be very flat and strong.

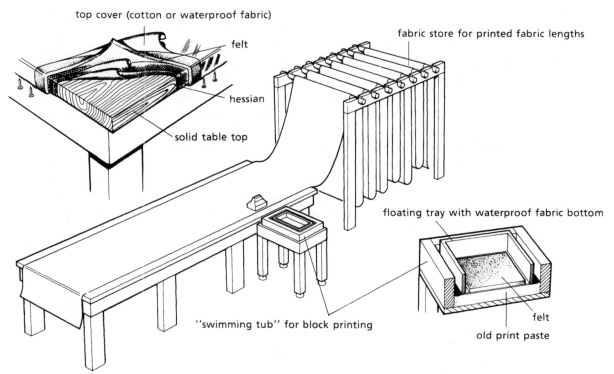

top cover (cotton or waterproof fabric)

felt

fabric store for printed fabric lengths

hessian

solid table top

floating tray with waterproof fabric bottom

"swimming tub" for block printing

felt

old print paste

Illustration 4 Block printing table and equipment

Screen printing can also be a relatively simple method of printing and again does not require the use of complex or expensive equipment, but a basic minimum makes things easier.

The simplest screen, usually called a stencil, is a flat sheet of waterproof paper or metal out of which a pattern has been cut. The dye is brushed or sprayed through the open areas on to the fabric. It has the defect that isolated areas fall out of the pattern and so limit the designs possible. If, however, the paper cut out is supported on a fine screen of woven yarns, it becomes possible to link isolated areas by the screen since the yarns are so fine that printing paste diffuses round them during printing. The simplest screen in this case is a frame covered with fine gauze which is used to support a paper pattern, the printing paste being forced through the open areas of the screen with a 'squeegee', or blade of wood or rubber, which is drawn across the screen to squeeze the printing paste through. Screens made in this way are very cheap but have a very short life. The pattern can also be produced directly on the screen gauze by hand painting with a suitable paint or lacquer which blocks out the portions which are not to be printed.

The screen can be prepared from a number of sources. It requires a frame, which can be of wood or metal, which is the correct size for the printing table and the fabric being printed. A suitable screen gauze is stretched tightly over the frame and fixed to the edge. Usually the size will allow the full width of the fabric being printed to be covered by one screen. As in block printing, each colour in the design needs one screen and the screens must be made so that the various colours 'fit' to form the final design. The screen gauze can be silk, cotton organdie, nylon, polyester, or phosphor bronze.

The most usual method these days is to prepare the pattern on the screen by photo-chemical methods: the screen gauze is coated with a light sensitive solution which is dried on the screen in the dark. The pattern to be printed is prepared separately by painting with a light-proof ink on translucent paper; a separate painting is needed for each colour in the design. The advantage is that these paintings can be prepared in a design studio away from the screen-making, with all the necessary equipment and care needed to make the various colours fit accurately. The painting is then placed over the prepared screen and exposed to light, which makes the light-sensitive portion become insoluble in water. When the screen is washed the unexposed portion is removed. By using modern sensitizing solutions this process becomes very quick and easy and the screens can have quite a long life, lasting for many printings. They can be made permanent by painting with a suitable waterproof lacquer. If a permanent screen is not needed and the screen gauze is made from a strong fibre such as polyester, it is possible to strip the screen coating and re-use the screen many times without the need to use fresh gauze.

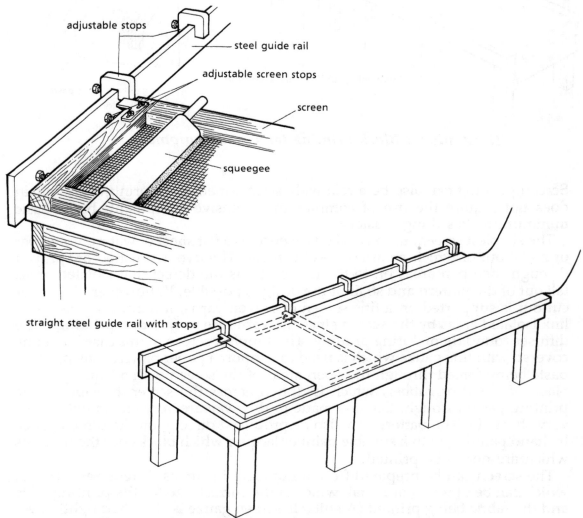

Illustration 5 Screen printing table and equipment

The printing table should be as shown in Illustration 5, and needs a flatter printing surface than is needed for block printing. The table also needs a very straight steel guide rail down one side which is used to locate the screens. The rail carries adjustable metal stops which are positioned at exactly the width of each repeat of the pattern. The screens are then located accurately over the fabric on the table by means of adjustable screws on the screen which make contact with the guide rail.

Some printing paste is poured into one end of the screen lying on the fabric and then drawn across the screen with the squeegee, forcing some paste through the open areas and on to the fabric. The screen is lifted and moved to the next-but-one position to avoid picking up wet paste from the first print, and so on until the first colour has been applied to the whole fabric. When this is completely dry the second colour is printed, and so on until the whole design is complete. The screens are washed, the fabric dried on the table or removed to dry, and then the print must be fixed.

Fixation

The aim is to create conditions which will allow the dye to be taken up by the fabric by forming a concentrated dyebath in the areas which have been printed. This is most often brought about by steaming the fabric, which provides the necessary heat and moisture. The type of steamer is very important if good dye fixation is to be achieved; it must provide a large volume of steam which is constantly replaced and which does not allow water to condense on the fabric. This is difficult to achieve with very simple steamers, which are likely to be used by small producers, but some types of printing are possible. Steaming is also an expensive operation, which is why some printing methods have been included in the Appendices which do not need steaming to bring about dye fixation.

Final treatments

These are dealt with in Appendix 2, but the aim must be to remove loose dye and thickening agents by a thorough washing. One problem for small producers is to bring this about without staining unprinted areas of the fabric. The most important aspect is to bring about the first wash as quickly as possible using as large a volume of water as possible. If a winch machine of the type shown in Illustration 12 (page 32) is available, this should be used.

This handbook can only give an outline of the general principles of dyeing and printing. For further details the reader is recommended to obtain some of the books and articles described in Chapter 7.

Working safely

Although most of the dyes and chemicals used in small-scale dyeing or printing are relatively safe, it is sensible to handle them carefully. A few common-sense precautions will make dyeing and printing a pleasant and safe occupation.

The most important safety measure is a clean and tidy working area. Every dye and chemical should have a clearly labelled container with a lid and its own place for storage. Nothing should be left lying about and if a container has been used to measure, say, acid it should never be left without rinsing carefully in case someone who does not know what it has been used for picks it up. Anything spilt should be cleaned up immediately and the cloth or mop used should be washed thoroughly. Avoid handling large storage containers: always transfer some of the chemical to a smaller container for use. Do not use concentrated solutions of acids:always make up a dilute solution for use in the dyehouse. Benches and floors should always be clean and free from obstructions. Dyebaths containing hot liquids should be supported securely, and beakers or other containers should not be heated on a bench but near to the floor.

Dye powders and dusty chemicals should be handled very carefully to avoid breathing the dust. Most dyes are now sold as non-dusting powders or grains, but for a very dusty substance wear a face mask. Once dyes or chemicals are wet they are not as unpleasant, but some dyes can be absorbed through the skin: wear gloves if possible and in any case do not allow the hands to become heavily dyed.

If strong chemicals are accidentally splashed on the skin or in the eyes, the safest treatment is to flood the area gently with a large volume of water: for the eyes this must be done by someone gently opening the eyelids. All such cases require medical attention as soon as possible. Make sure that the hospital or doctor knows what treatment has been given.

Food or drink should not be stored, prepared, or eaten in any room containing dyes or chemicals. Hands should always be washed after dyeing and before eating. Smoking can be extremely dangerous near to dyes or chemicals.

Protective clothing is very useful in the dyehouse. A strong waterproof apron is useful and thick waterproof gloves are essential when handling hot yarn or fabrics in the dyeing machines. The floor in a dyehouse inevitably is almost always wet. Waterproof boots should be worn and in a hot climate plastic slip-on shoes are useful. Bare feet should be discouraged.

3. SIMPLE METHODS OF TESTING

TESTING AND QUALITY CONTROL

The quality of dyed or printed materials, apart from obvious defects such as uneven dyeing or bad printing, is usually indicated by the fastness of the materials — the resistance which the dye or print possesses to removal or change, either during normal processing, e.g. washing after printing, or in use, e.g. fading in daylight. All dyes or pigments will eventually change in use. Sometimes this change is seen simply as an apparent loss of colour, but it may also be accompanied by a change of shade.

Colour fastness, particularly to fading in daylight, is not solely a property of an individual dye but also depends upon which fibre the dye is applied to: the same dye will have a different fastness when used on cotton compared to linen, or wool compared to silk. Colour fastness also depends upon the depth of the dyeing or print. Deep shades have a higher light fastness than pale shades, but usually less washing fastness.

For these and other reasons, internationally accepted standards have been set up for all colour fastness testing, both for the depth of shade at which testing is carried out and for the conditions used in the tests. Most of these tests require special equipment and materials to be carried out successfully, and it is unlikely that anyone outside a properly established textile testing laboratory could undertake them. If an acceptable standard measure of the fastness of any dyeing or print is required for any reason, this must be obtained from a properly equipped testing laboratory.

However, some simple comparative tests are still possible in which the quality of a dyeing or print can be compared with one which has proved to be satisfactory in use. Such tests are very useful as a method of quality control, but of course the results are only of use in the particular situation in which they are carried out and cannot be compared with the results of tests carried out in a different place or using different testing conditions.

Testing should be undertaken to ensure that the fastness properties of whatever is being dyed or printed is suitable for the product for which it is intended. If a manufacturer's pattern card is available for the dyes which are being used, an indication of the light fastness and wet fastness of the dyes on the card will usually be given. Some dyes, even in the same dye group, will be seen to have a much higher resistance to fading or removal than others and it is important to choose dyes which are most suitable for the product being made: good light fastness for articles which are to be used mostly out of doors, good wet fastness for those which will be washed frequently, etc. If mixtures of dyes are being used to match a particular colour, it is important, if possible, to choose dyes with similar light fastness, so that an unacceptable change of colour does not take place in use. The figures given by the dye manufacturer were obtained by testing the dye under the standard conditions, but nevertheless are a useful indication of the fastness properties which can be expected. However, any dye may apparently give very different results when tested by a different method, and it is always best to test under conditions which will eventually be encountered.

Testing should be carried out for new dyeings or prints where there could be some uncertainty about the fastness. However, provided that dyeing or printing conditions have not been changed, or a new dye is not being used, it is unnecessary to test all dyeings or prints undertaken with a dye with known good fastness properties.

References are given in Chapter 7 to sources of information about recognized methods for fastness testing. The figures given in manufacturers' pattern cards, which are obtained as a result of carrying out the standard tests, are intended to indicate how fast, in numerical terms, a particular dyeing or print is in relation to both the test and other dyes tested by the same method. The two most important fastness tests are:

1 Fastness to light, in the range:

> 1 = Very poor
> 2 = Poor
> 3 = Moderate
> 4 = Fairly good
> 5 = Good
> 6 = Very good
> 7 = Excellent
> 8 = Outstanding

2 Fastness to washing or water, in the range:

> 1 = Poor
> 2 = Moderate
> 3 = Fairly good
> 4 = Good
> 5 = Very good

Fastness to water and washing

This test can be used to determine if a dyeing will lose colour on contact with water or on washing, or if the dyed or printed material will stain other materials with which it comes into contact. Two tests should always be carried out in the same conditions, one for the dyeing under test and one for a dyeing whose properties are known to be satisfactory.

If the loss of colour and degree of staining is much worse than for a dyeing known to be satisfactory, then an alternative dye or mixture of dyes should be tested.

Fabrics of wool and cotton have been chosen for the test because they are the two materials likely to be used most often in, for example clothing, but two pieces of cotton will be satisfactory, or cotton and polyester. The fabrics used should be the ones with which the dyeing or print is most likely to come into contact in use.

Fastness to other treatments

The same principles can be applied to other treatments which the dyed material is likely to meet during processing or use.

Fastness to water

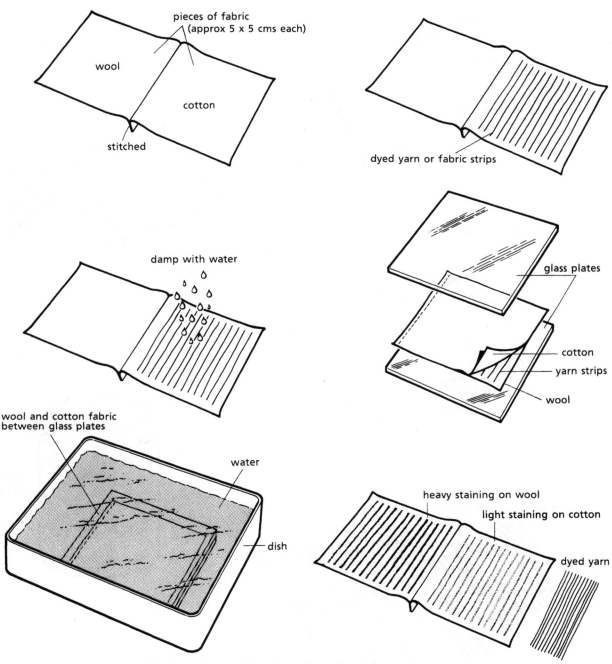

Illustration 6 Testing dye fastness to water

(1)   Take two pieces of cloth about 5 cm by 5 cm one of which is undyed wool and the other undyed cotton and stitch them together along one side.
(2)   Take a portion of the dyed or printed material to be tested, several strands of yarn or strips of printed material, and spread this evenly between the two pieces of cloth as in the diagram.
(3)   Wet the fabrics with clean cold water (preferably distilled).
(4)   Fold the two pieces of fabric together to enclose the material being tested and place them between two glass plates as shown.
(5)   Place the fabrics in a dish and cover with clean cold water (preferably distilled). Press the top piece of glass gently to remove bubbles and leave for 15 mins.
(6)   Without disturbing the plates, pour off the water from the dish and then leave the plates for 4 hours.
(7)   Remove the fabrics, open them, and remove the dyed yarn or fabric. Allow them to dry in air.

How to examine:

(8)   Place the dyed yarn or fabric next to a sample which has not been tested and compare the change which has taken place with the sample of a satisfactory dyeing tested at the same time. If the dyeing or print being tested shows equal or less change then it is as good as the satisfactory sample.
(9)   Place the wool and cotton cloths next to samples of the same materials which have not been tested and compare them with cloths which have been tested with a satisfactory dyeing. Equal or less staining shows equal or better fastness.

Fastness to washing

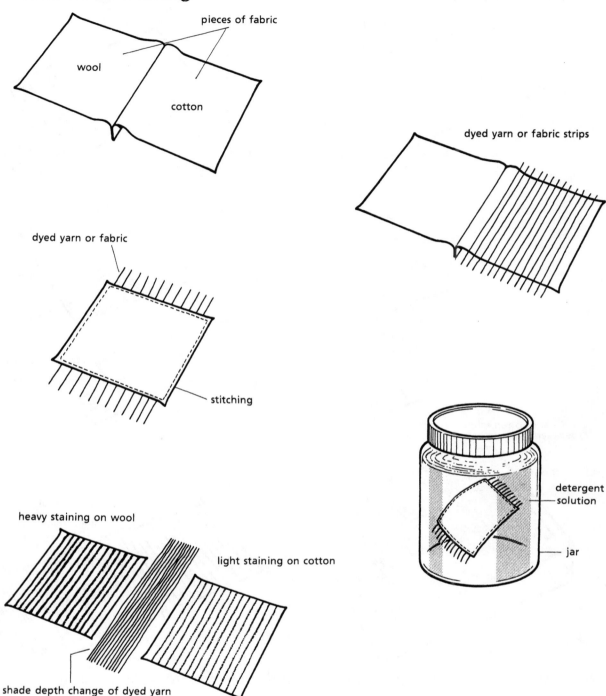

Illustration 7 Testing dye fastness to washing

(1) Take two pieces of cloth about 5 cm by 5 cm one of which is undyed wool and the other undyed cotton and stitch them together along one side.
(2) Take a portion of the dyed or printed material to be tested, several strands of yarn or strips of printed fabric, and spread them evenly between the two pieces of cloth so that they overlap the sides as in the diagram.
(3) Sew around all four sides so that the yarn or strips are held in place. If dyed loose fibre is being tested, a combed layer can be placed between the fabrics.
(4) Prepare a similar specimen with dyed material which has satisfactory properties and place them in two jars with screw lids containing a solution of 5 gm per litre soap or detergent solution at 30°C. (The solution can be chosen to represent the conditions which the dyed material will have to withstand in use.)
(5) Agitate the two jars gently for 30 mins, then remove the fabrics and wash them in clean water for 5 mins. Open the stitching and separate the pieces to dry in air.
(6) Examine as for the test for water fastness.

Fastness to light

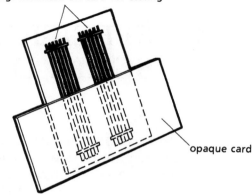

dyeings mounted on card for testing

opaque card

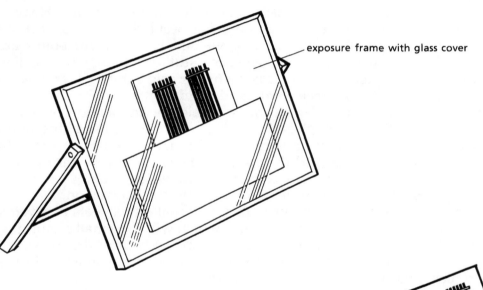

exposure frame with glass cover

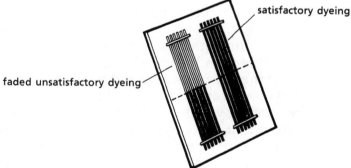

satisfactory dyeing

faded unsatisfactory dyeing

Illustration 8 Testing dye fastness to daylight

(1) Take a bundle of dyed fibre or yarn or strip of printed material about 5 cm long, and place it on a card next to a similar bundle of fibres which are known to have a satisfactory light fastness.
(2) Fix the fibres to the card and cover half with another piece of card or aluminium foil as in the diagram.
(3) Place the card on a frame covered by a piece of glass so that it faces the midday sun and is mounted at about 45°. The glass should be about 5 cm from the card so that air can circulate freely but rain is kept out.
(4) Examine the card daily until there is a sharp contrast between the exposed and unexposed portions. If it is desired to know how the dye fades over the short and long term, further portions can be covered at given intervals of time.
(5) If after exposure the dyeing or print shows the same degree of fading as the satisfactory sample, that is, the same contrast between the exposed and unexposed portions, the dye is satisfactory.

4. SPECIFICATIONS OF SMALL-SCALE DYEING MACHINES

1 Materials for construction

Fortunately, most dyeing machines for treating small quantities of material by hand can be very simple. If the dyeing machine needs to be heated directly by a fire or gas flame, it must be constructed of metal. Many dyes are affected by the presence of iron or copper in the water, so it is not possible to use these metals in an untreated state to make dyevats. Stainless steel is the best construction metal but is very expensive and difficult to fabricate. Heavily galvanized steel has proved successful, although it is best if the vat is constructed before galvanizing, if possible, so that any welded joints or cut edges are properly treated. Galvanized vats are most successful for dyeing with alkaline solutions, as in cotton dyeing, but are less useful for acid solutions, as in wool dyeing, as the acid tends to attack joints and welds.

If the vat is heated indirectly, by steam or by electric immersion heater, it can be made of enamelled steel, glazed pottery, concrete, high-melting-point plastic, or wood. Wood is a useful construction material but must be used with care. It absorbs dye very easily and the vat must be cleaned very thoroughly between dyeings or used for only one colour. Whichever material is used, any openings for pipes or drains must also not be subject to corrosion.

Few large manufacturers of dyeing machines now make small vats for dyeing by hand. They do make 'laboratory' machines which will dye small quantities, but in general these are designed to imitate, on a small scale, conditions which exist in the large machines and so tend to be complex and expensive. In the situations which this handbook is designed to help, it is assumed that the dyevats will be made locally, or improvised from suitable existing products: old washing machines can be a useful source of containers which often contain an immersion heater. However, it is generally best to make the dyevat, since it can then be of the size and type required in a particular situation. The drawings and specifications which follow are all intended for local manufacture and can be made by any workshop with simple sheet metal bending and welding equipment, although joints can be riveted if welding is not possible. All the vats rely upon moving the material to be dyed through the dyevat by hand, although power operation could be used on some fabric dyeing machines.

2 Form in which the material is dyed

Textile materials will usually be dyed as loose fibre, yarn, or fabric. The simple rectangular dyevat shown in Illustration 9 is probably the most useful 'universal' dyeing machine since it can be made from a wide variety of materials and can be used to dye loose fibre, yarns in hanks, and short pieces of fabric. It is also useful for the production of tie-dye and other effects on yarns and fabrics. Straight sticks of wood or suitable metal can be used to move the loose fibre through the vat, or hold the hanks of yarn during dyeing. Bent sticks as shown are useful when dyeing hanks, which should always be under the surface of

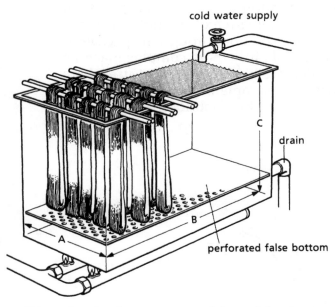

Direct heating by gas or wood in metal vat

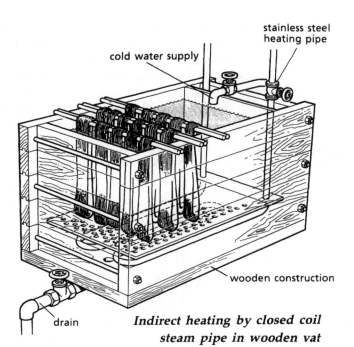

Indirect heating by closed coil steam pipe in wooden vat

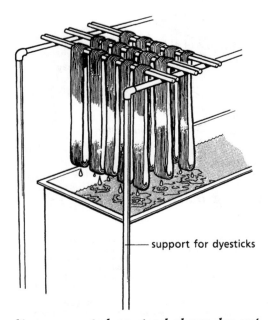

Yarn supported on stand above dye vat

Bent sticks used as an alternative to straight

Illustration 9 Universal dyebath

GENERAL DESCRIPTION

The dyebath should be constructed in a suitable material not subject to corrosion and not containing copper or any copper-containing alloy. If the vat is heated directly over a fire or by gas burner, it must be of stainless steel or heavily galvanized steel. If heated indirectly by electric immersion heater or steam it can also be made of wood, glazed pottery, enamelled steel or high melting point plastic. It is essential that all joints or openings for pipework or heaters are themselves not subject to corrosion and do not contain copper.

(1)   Dimension A should be of sufficient width to take two or three hanks of yarn evenly spread on a stick: this is the maximum quantity of wet yarn which can be conveniently handled. Any increase in size of dyebath should then only take place by an increase in dimension B.

(2)   Size of bath should reflect average dyelot, 10lb (4.5 kg) seems to be the average but it would also be useful to have at least another size, say for 30lb (14kg). The larger dyebath would be more or less a fixture and would require a drain for emptying.

(3)   With a perforated false bottom dimension C is not critical but should be about three-quarters of the hank length.

(4)   If the vat is heated indirectly by steam, direct injection from a perforated pipe is the quickest method, but this causes considerable condensation in the vat with a consequent increase in liquor volume. Heating by a closed steam coil is therefore more successful for the smaller dyevats.

(5)   Dyesticks should be both straight, for most dyeing methods, and bent for vat dyeing.

(6)   The perforated false bottom should be easily removable for cleaning purposes.

(7)   The simple open design of the dyevat means that it can also be used as a general purpose vat for the production of tie-dye and other effects on both yarns and fabrics.

(8)   For 5-10lb yarn A = 16 inches (41cm); B = 28 inches (71 cm); C = 23 inches (58 cm). The perforated false bottom should be 2½ inches (6cm) from the bottom of the vat.

the dye solution as in vat dyeing. Dyeing yarn in some type of 'package', such as a cheese or cone, is not described, since this requires a more complex machine which usually needs a pump to circulate the dye solution through the packages.

Fabrics, other than very short pieces, need a slightly more complex machine to operate successfully. The two types which are likely to be most useful are winch and jig machines. Winch machines, an example of which is shown in Illustration 10, are most useful for dyeing short lengths of fabric, of any material.

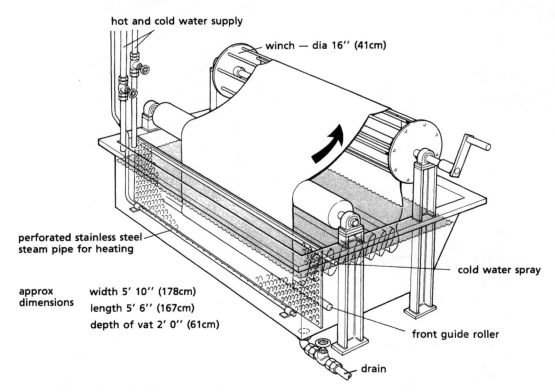

Illustration 10 Winch fabric dyeing machine

GENERAL DESCRIPTION
The dyebath should be constructed in a suitable material not subject to corrosion and not containing copper or any copper-containing alloy. If the vat is heated directly over a fire or a gas burner it must be of stainless steel or heavily galvanized steel. If heated indirectly it can also be made of wood. Because of the size it is strongly recommended that heating by steam injection from a perforated pipe should be used if possible. If direct heating is used a perforated false bottom must be incorporated in the vat. All joints or openings for pipework must be not subject to corrosion.
(1)   The dimensions of the winch are not critical but the size indicated in the drawing is sufficiently wide to allow many fabrics to be dyed at open width. This is sometimes necessary for fairly heavy fabrics which might be subject to creasing; if the winch is too narrow, fabrics must always be dyed in rope form.
(2)   The size of machine in the drawing will allow up to 40 metres of medium weight cotton fabric to be dyed at open width and about this amount of light cotton in two ropes. The same quantities would of course apply when the machine is used for fabric preparation. To increase the machine capacity the depth should be increased.
(3)   The winch can be driven by hand or by an electric motor (waterproof). The speed should be approximately 30 RPM which will necessitate a reduction gearbox if a motor is used.
(4)   All pipework feeding the winch with water etc. must be of suitable dimensions: 2 inch supply pipes are necessary and the drain should be 3 inches for quick emptying.
(5)   All joints and internal surfaces in the vat which might come into contact with fabric must be smooth and free from projections of any kind.
(6)   The perforated steam pipe for heating and the cold water spray pipe must be stainless steel in the vat. Connections to these pipes and other supply pipes can be of normal steel.
(7)   Bearings for the winch and guide roller can be plain with grease point or ball bearings.

The fabrics are sewn on to the machine in a continuous length, either in the form of a 'rope', that is, the fabric is allowed to bunch together, or at open width in which the fabric is held at full width during dyeing. Roping the fabric is most successful for lightweight and knitted fabrics and running the fabric at open width for heavier fabrics or those which might be subject to creasing during dyeing. Most dyeing takes place whilst the fabric moves slowly through the dyevat, a short length being constantly turned over the winch. It is important, therefore, that conditions in the dyevat are as even as possible so

30

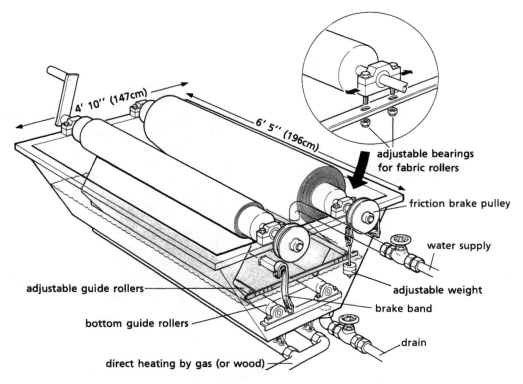

Illustration 11 Hand-operated jig dyeing machine

GENERAL DESCRIPTION
The dyebath should be constructed of a suitable material not subject to corrosion and not containing copper or any copper-containing alloy. If the vat is heated directly by wood or gas it must be of stainless steel or heavily galvanized sheet steel. If heated indirectly it can be of wood. It is strongly recommended that the heating should be by a perforated steam pipe if this is possible. All joints or openings in the vat for pipe work should be corrosion resistant.
(1)   The dimensions given will take most fabrics up to 48 inches wide and about 60-250 metres in length depending on the weight of the fabric.
(2)   The braking mechanism for the fabric rollers is essential and should be adjusted for each dyeing so that the fabric runs evenly without creasing but with the minimum possible tension.
(3)   The adjustable guide rollers should be positioned according to the amount of fabric being dyed so that it again runs as smoothly as possible.
(4)   If the fabric lengths are joined together to make up a batch for dyeing, they must be butt-joined by very careful stitching.
(5)   The bearings for the bottom guide rollers should be waterproof plain or ball bearings.
(6)   The brake band can be a leather strap running in the groove in the brake pulley.
(7)   If a perforated steam pipe is used for heating it should be of stainless steel. Connections to it can be of normal steel pipe.
(8)   Fabric rollers must be exactly parallel and there must be a small adjustment built in to the bearing mounts of one roller. Normally oval bolt holes are sufficient. The same applies for the bottom guide rollers.

that the fabric does not dye unevenly. The front guide roller is important in this respect to ensure that the fabric does not float across the surface of the vat but is forced under the surface of the dye solution.

The jig, shown in Illustration 11, is the classic machine for dyeing cotton, or indeed for preparing fabric for dyeing. It is not suited to dyeing wool fabrics, since the fabric is always under tension during dyeing. Fabrics are always at open width and, in this case, most dyeing takes place whilst the fabric is on the rollers since it passes through the dyevat very quickly. This means that all additions to the vat, dyes and chemicals, must be made in equal portions at the beginning of each consecutive passage of the fabric from one roller to the other (known as an 'end') and an equal number of ends is always given. It is also important that fabrics should be of even width throughout the length and that selvages should be even, as any uneven widths will dye differently at the edges. If fabrics are joined together for dyeing to make a certain length, the joints must be butt sewn if they are not to show after dyeing. All this means that the jig is most successful as a dyeing machine for fabrics made on a power loom: handloom fabrics must be extremely even to dye without problems.

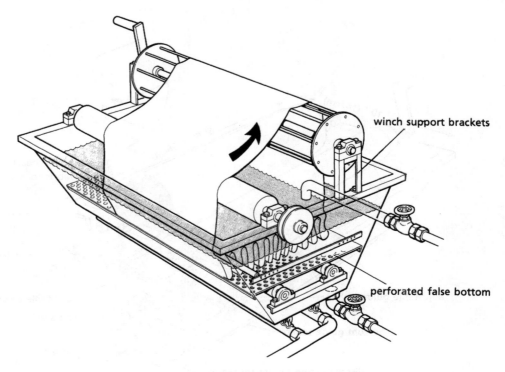

winch support brackets

perforated false bottom

Illustration 12 Conversion of jig to operate as winch

(1)   To convert to winch, lift off one fabric roller and bolt on support brackets.
(2)   Place winch and shaft on bearings on the support brackets. The shaft should have a handle at one end, but no brake roller at the other.
(3)   Position the winch so that the fabric has a straight drop into the dyebath.
(4)   It may prove necessary to have a perforated false bottom resting on the bottom guide rollers when operating as a winch.

The jig can be modified to operate as a winch by removing one fabric roller
and replacing it with a winch as shown in Illustration 12.

5. PLANNING FOR PRODUCTION

The type of planning needed will depend upon the scale of production of dyed and printed materials, whether on a very small scale, as an adjunct to an existing weaving or knitting operation, or on a slightly larger scale with a centralized dyehouse serving a number of spinning, weaving, or knitting units. Printing is slightly more difficult to organize on a very small scale. Even a small number of printing tables will require quite a large and regular supply of fabrics for printing, and the supply of dyes and chemicals to support this activity usually requires a central organization to be effective.

Both printing and dyeing are textile activities with a relatively rapid turnround for finished articles, unlike spinning. Even a small and simple dyehouse will be able to handle the requirements of a large number of spinners and weavers for dyed fibre and yarn, and will be able to process a fairly large volume of woven or knitted fabrics if fabric dyeing is a part of the operation.

For these reasons it is generally best if dyeing and printing are organized in a more centralized manner with a small dyehouse serving a district. The activities of dyeing and printing can of course be organized on any scale, but on a very small scale some of the advantages of centralization can be lost, such as bulk buying for dyes and chemicals, the provision of services such as heating and water, and the use of trained personnel with specialized knowledge of the processes.

Most of this chapter is therefore concerned with the establishment and running of a small dyeing and/or printing activity which is designed to handle the requirements of an area for dyed fibre, yarn, or fabric and has the capacity to print a reasonable quantity of fabric on a regular basis. The dyeing and printing techniques described in this handbook are of course applicable whatever the size of the operation.

Basic requirements

The most important requirement is probably an adequate supply of good quality water. Even a fairly small dyehouse, with one or two small-capacity vats and a dyeing machine for fabric, will require several thousand gallons of water per day for dyeing, washing, etc. The water must be of good quality, not heavily contaminated with dissolved salts such as iron and not strongly coloured. There should also be an adequate flow of water: a steady supply from one or two small taps will not be sufficient, nor will a supply which must be pumped by hand from a tube well. Some form of reservoir for the water is useful, either storage tanks or a stream dam, from which the dyehouse can be supplied by large-diameter piping. Obviously there should be a regular supply throughout the year.

Good heating is important. If it is inadequate dyeing becomes prolonged and the productive capacity of the dyehouse is reduced. Direct heating of the dyevats by wood or gas is possible, but there must obviously be an adequate supply of wood, which may be expensive, and gas burners must be of an adequate size to heat the dyevats quickly. Direct heating by electric immersion heaters is usually too expensive. Indirect heating is very effective, usually by steam raised from a gas-fired or wood-burning boiler; the steam can be injected directly into the vats or circulated through a closed coil heating system. This is probably the most effective way of providing heating for a dyehouse, if it can be arranged, and has the added advantage that the steam can also be used for steaming printed fabrics for dye fixation.

A good supply of high quality dyes and chemicals is essential. If these are supplied by a local merchant, there can sometimes be problems with quality. Most of the large dye manufacturers maintain offices in almost every country in the world and these are a source of information and will usually also supply lists of reliable merchants selling their products. Use them. A list of addresses of the principal dye manufacturers is included in Chapter 6.

If dyeing or printing is being introduced as a new activity to an area, or if an unusual dyeing or printing process is being recommended, suitable training should be considered an essential first step, even if this is only for one or two key personnel. The training programme should include discussions with all those who might be involved with the new activity and also with all those who might be affected by it, such as weavers or spinners or design staff, who can thus make their particular requirements known at an early stage. Any training programme must also include the safety aspects of using new and perhaps unfamiliar equipment and chemicals. Suitable training is sometimes available at major textile centres or educational institutions in the area.

Before making any decisions about the scale or type of equipment needed in a particular situation, the points in the standard check list should be carefully considered:

COST Is there sufficient justification or need for the level of expenditure planned? Is there sufficient cash available to meet purchase costs? If money is borrowed for purchases, can it be repaid satisfactorily? Are there any local or government supported loan schemes to cover the capital cost of equipment or for the cost of establishing small industries? Is sufficient cash available to meet day-to-day running expenses, wages, work in progress, and stocks?

CAPACITY Does the choice of dyeing or printing equipment meet the desired production of dyed or printed products and the availability of materials for dyeing? Is there room for expansion? Is the type of equipment specified sufficiently flexible to meet all the known or projected needs of the dyehouse for at least five years?

LOCATION If a centralized dyehouse or printing unit is planned, will this arrangement meet the known needs of the particular situation most successfully? Would a more decentralized arrangement be better? If so is suitable transport available at reasonable cost to move materials, and will suitable training be needed and available?

AVAILABILITY Is the proposed equipment available locally from a reputable manufacturer or can it be made locally? Are manufacturing instructions available and are there sufficient local skills to carry out construction? What kind of spare parts and maintenance service is available? If power-driven equipment is planned, is a reliable power supply available for a reasonable period each day?

EXPERIENCE Is the equipment easy to use? Can tuition in dyeing and printing be obtained locally or at a national training centre? What local skills exist or could be trained for maintaining the equipment?

SOCIAL ACCEPTABILITY Will local people readily accept the equipment and methods of working which are planned? Will there be any changes to existing social practice caused by the introduction of new processes and working methods? Has the demand for change come from the local community or from outside?

After shortlisting the most suitable range of equipment, an economic evaluation of all inputs and outgoings associated with it will help to identify the best final choice. Finally, seek expert advice about the equipment and how it is proposed to use it before going ahead with purchase or manufacture.

Economics of dyeing and printing yarn and fabric

Once a dyeing and printing operation has been planned in some detail, it is a useful exercise to examine the likely cost of dyeing yarn or printing fabric to give a rough idea of the viability of the proposed operation. Dyeing is of course only one of the many operations required from raw materials to the finished textile product, and dyeing or printing costs will be only a small proportion of the final product cost. Nevertheless it is best if initial costings are made on the actual cost of dyeing even if the activity is carried out as part of a larger operation, and it is obviously very important if it is intended that the dyeing shall be undertaken on a commission basis.

The cost of any textile activity, including dyeing, has two components, overheads (fixed or indirect costs), and variable (direct costs).

Indirect costs
1 Interest on the cost of any raw materials (dyes, chemicals, yarn or fabric if working on commission)
2 Cost of premises
3 Heat/light/power for premises
4 Telephone
5 Cost of depreciation on equipment and interest on any loans for purchase
6 Consumable materials
7 Insurance
8 Postage/stationery

Direct costs
1 Raw materials (dyes, chemicals, heating for dyebaths)
2 Wastage (yarn and fabric spoiled in dyeing and printing)
3 Transport
4 Wages (including any contribution to a welfare fund and any incentive wages)

(The cost of dyeing and printing should include all processing, preparation of yarn and fabric and any aftertreatment, as well as the cost of water.)

Once an estimate of production has been made for the planned dyehouse or printing unit, the costs can be worked out for, say, one week's production. The actual dyeing cost per unit of material dyed is then the weekly indirect costs plus the weekly direct costs divided by the number of units of material dyed or printed. To this cost must be added an agreed profit per unit to give an actual selling price.

A simple plan is given for a small dyehouse and a printing unit. The dyehouse contains two yarn dyeing vats and a fabric dyeing machine which can operate as a winch or jig.

This would have a maximum output of dyed yarn of 27 kg/day, with an average of 15 kg. The fabric dyeing machine would have a maximum output as a jig of 280 metres/day, with an average of 90m. When operated as a winch it would have a maximum output of 55 metres/day with an average of 27m.

The outputs given depend to a large extent on how the dyehouse is organized and upon the skills of the staff working in it. If, for example, colour matching is an important consideration and the staff are not very experienced, output can be greatly reduced. The output can also be reduced if heating is inefficient and slow, if the water flow is too slow, and if the daily workload for the dyehouse is not properly organized. Since two people are required to operate each dyevat, maximum output would be possible with six personnel. Experience has also shown that maximum efficiency can be obtained if one person at least is trained and skilled in colour matching and is responsible for organizing the daily work, making up dye solutions, and generally controlling the operation. With correct operation it should be possible to produce at least two dyeings per day from each machine.

Siting of the dyehouse is important. It is obviously best on the ground floor if in a building, with easy access for materials. Good ventilation is essential, particularly if the dyevats are heated directly by wood or gas: in the former case the dyehouse is best situated in the open with a simple roof and open sides. Concrete is the best material for the floor, with open drains to take away the inevitable spillage and keep the floor reasonably dry. The disposal of the effluent produced by the dyehouse must be carefully considered: even a small dyehouse such as the one described will produce about 2000 gallons of effluent per day when in full operation, and much of this may be highly coloured. Details of any national or local regulations covering the disposal of industrial effluents should be obtained from the appropriate authority. This problem is discussed in more detail in Appendix 10.

The dyehouse may also be used for the preparation and aftertreatment of printed fabrics where printing is undertaken on the same site. There are distinct advantages when dyeing and printing are undertaken as part of the same operation. The dyehouse can prepare and dye fabrics for printing and wash them after printing. If a steam-raising boiler is used for indirect heating in the dyehouse, it can also be used to steam fabrics after printing. Where long lengths of fabric are prepared and dyed on, for example, a dye jig, it is useful to have a small four-wheel flat truck to transport the wet fabric.

Small dyehouse

1   The situation should be carefully considered. The dyehouse is always best if it can have a concrete floor with drains, as in Illustration 13. Access should be easy so that trolleys of wet fabric and yarn can be moved in and out without difficulty. The drain should lead directly to a pond or settling tank (see Appendix 10).

2   If a piped water supply can be arranged, the pipework should be of suitable dimensions: 2 inch supply pipes and drainage valves are necessary for quick filling and emptying.

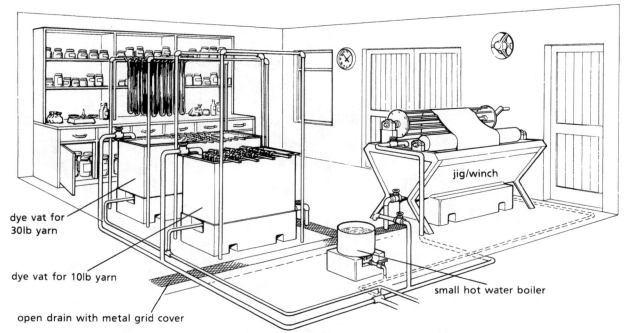

dye vat for
30lb yarn

dye vat for 10lb yarn

open drain with metal grid cover

jig/winch

small hot water boiler

Illustration 13 Small dyehouse for yarn and fabric dyeing

3   The gas burners should be dimensioned to give quick heating. If wood is used for heating, an open-sided dyehouse is best. In both cases the dyevats are mounted on brick or mud plinths.

4   Good ventilation is important:with all machines in operation an enclosed room can become very hot.

5   A small extra gas burner or mud stove is useful for heating small quantities of water, boiling up dye solutions, etc.

6   The shelving is used for storing jars of dye. The bench is used to hold scales and measures:a large-capacity scale is needed to weigh the material to be dyed, a small-capacity scale (accuracy 0.010 gm) is needed to weigh out dyes and other chemicals. Large tubs for storing bulk chemicals such as salt can be stored under the bench.

7   Each dyevat can be calibrated with a dipstick by measuring the capacity the first time the vat is filled. Two or three graduated measures for small quantities of liquid are useful.

Small printing unit

1   Fabrics will need to be prepared for printing and washed after printing, and so the printing unit should be situated close to the dyehouse. If this is not possible, and printing must be undertaken in a different place, extra transport costs are incurred and the types of printing possible are limited. Because of the variety of available methods, it is not possible to give more than an indication of the basic elements necessary to carry out block or screen printing and these are shown in the illustration. The arrangement of the elements is not critical, but experience has shown that they work best under one roof.

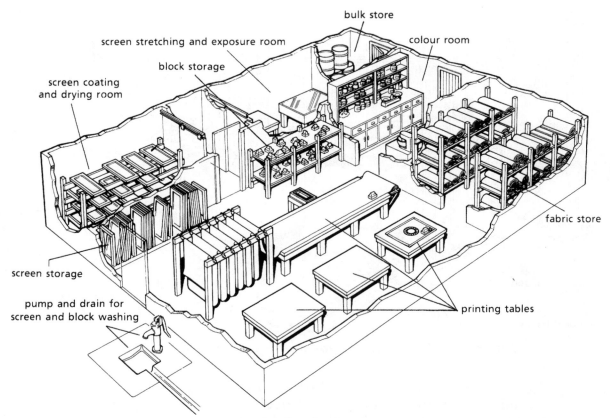

Illustration 14 Small printing unit for block and screen printing

2   The printing area should be light and airy, with plenty of working space round the tables. The tables should be sized according to what is being printed, and be of extremely solid construction, with a very flat printing surface and a slightly resilient cover.

3   The colour room should contain plenty of bench area, storage for dyes and pigments, bulk storage areas under the benches. Weighing scales and liquid measures are necessary, and a small gas burner useful, for making solutions. A high-speed mixer is essential for pigment printing. A sink with tap is useful.

4   Bulk storage of inflammable liquids such as kerosene or white spirit should be in a separate store.

5   If screen-printing is intended, a darkroom fitted with an orange safelight is needed for screen-making.

6. EQUIPMENT AND MATERIALS SUPPLIERS

Dyeing equipment

United Kingdom
Most of the large manufacturers of dyeing equipment no longer make small dyeing machines suitable for use by hand. They do sometimes make fairly small machines, but these usually require a supply of electricity or steam for operation. If these are required they can be approached.

Longclose Ltd, Dewsbury Road, Leeds, W. Yorks. LS11 5LH.
Pegg-Whitely Ltd, New Star Road Works, Leicester, LE4 7LP.
T. Bibby Ltd, Jasper Street, Queens Road, Halifax, W. Yorks, HX1 4NT.
Metal Fabrications, Nile Terrace, Trafalgar Avenue, Peckham, London SE15 6NS.

Most of the dyeing machines described in this handbook are very simple and can be made by any competent workshop accustomed to sheet metal work.

Printing equipment

United Kingdom
The following companies can supply a wide range of equipment suitable for a small-scale printing operation, from printing tables to steamers.

The Macclesfield Engineering Co. Ltd
Windmill Street
Macclesfield
Cheshire SK11 7HS.

Adelphi Engineering and Sheet Metal Co.
Grimshaw Lane
Bollington
Cheshire SK11 2QR.

Ellis Jones & Co. Ltd
Tiviot Colour Works
Stockport SK4 1UR.

Metal Fabrications
Nile Terrace
Trafalgar Avenue
Peckham
London SE15 6NS.

A. J. Purdey & Co. Ltd
248 Lea Bridge Road
Leyton
London E10.

Screen Process Supplies Ltd
24 Parsons Green Lane
London SW6 4HS.

Dyestuff manufacturers or their agents

Amritlal Chemaux Ltd
Rang Vdyan
Sitladevi Temple Road
Mahim
Bombay 400 016
India

Atul Products Ltd
PO Atul
Valsad 396 020
Gujarat
India

Ciba-Geigy AG
CH-4002 Basel
Switzerland
(Abbreviated CGY)

Bayer AG
D-5090 Leverkusen-Bayerwerk
Federal Republic of Germany

Hoechst AG
ATA Geschaftsbereich D/Fabern
Postfach 80 03 20
6230 Frankfurt/M 80
Federal Republic of Germany
(Abbreviated HOE)

India Dyestuff Industries Ltd
Mafatlal Centre
Nariman Point
Bombay 400 021
India

Holliday Dyes and Chemicals Ltd
PO Box B22
Leeds Road
Deighton
Huddersfield HD2 1UH
UK

Cassella AG
Hanauer Landstrasse 526
PO Box 6000
Frankfurt/M61
Federal Republic of Germany

Chemiequip Ltd
501 Embassy Centre
Nariman Point
Bombay 400 021
India

BASF AG
Carl Boschstrasse 38
D-6700 Ludwigshafen
Federal Republic of Germany

Dylon International Ltd
Worsley Bridge Road
Lower Sydenham
London SE26 5HD
UK

Imperial Chemical Industries plc
PO Box 42
Hexagon House
Blackley
Manchester M9 3DA
UK
(Abbreviated ICI)

Nippon Kagaku Co. Ltd
Tokyo
Japan

Yorkshire Chemicals plc
Kirkstall Road
Leeds LS3 1LL
UK

Chemical manufacturers or agents

Cargo Fleet Chemical Co. Ltd
Eaglescliffe Industrial Estate
Eaglescliffe
Stockton-on-Tees
Cleveland TS16 OPN
UK
(Agents for products of ICI
Petrochemicals Division, e.g.
Synperonic BD)

Durham Chemicals Distributors Ltd
55-57 Glengall Road
London SE15 6NQ
UK

Textile Dyestuffs and Chemicals Ltd
Cliffe Road
Brighouse
West Yorkshire HD6 1HD
UK

Midand Dyechem Ltd
1 St Ives Road
Leicester LE4 7FL
UK

Rudolf and Co. KG
Spreestrasse 3-7
Postfach 749
D-8192 Geretaried 2
Federal Republic of Germany

Mathieson Dyes & Chemicals
Marcon Place
London E8 1LP
UK

Albright and Wilson Ltd
Industrial Chemicals Division
PO Box 3, Oldbury
Warley, Worcs B68 0NN
UK

Allied Colloids Ltd
PO Box 38
Low Moor
Bradford
W Yorks BD12 OJZ
UK

Testing equipment

United Kingdom

Goodbrand-Jeffreys Ltd
Elm Works Mere Lane
Rochdale
Manchester OL11 3TE
UK

Shirley Developments Ltd
856 Wilmslow Road
Didsbury
Manchester M20 8SA
UK

James Heal and Co. Ltd
Richmond Works
Lake View
Halifax
W. Yorks HX3 6EP
UK

Mixing equipment

Joshua Greaves and Sons Ltd
Ramsbottom
Bury
Lancs BL0 9BA
UK

7. SOURCES OF FURTHER INFORMATION

Most of the organizations mentioned below are useful sources of information. If detailed information is needed it is often important to know which department or individual to approach.

1   Research organizations. Many have information services which are available even to non-members.

2   Other useful sources of information including institutions, federations, and guilds.

3   Written sources of information. This includes a selected list of publications used in the compilation of this manual.

Research organizations

(a)   They almost always have an information service on a wide range of textile topics. This usually includes book lists and copies of research papers.

(b)   They will usually undertake testing or other work for which a charge is made.

(c)   They sometimes organize courses or training programmes in aspects of textile manufacture.

United Kingdom

Wira, Wira House, West Park Ring Road, Leeds LS16 6QL
Tel. 0532 718381. Telex 557189

International Wool Secretariat, Technical Centre, Valley Drive, Ilkley, LS29 8PB.
Tel. 0943 601555. Telex 51457

Shirley Institute, Didsbury, Manchester, M20 8RX
Tel. 061 445 8141. Telex 668417

India

The South India Textile Research Association (SITRA)
Coimbatore 641014, Tamil Nadu

Ahmedabad Textile Industry Research Association (ATIRA)
Polytechnic Post Office, Ahmedabad 380015, Gujarat

Textile and Allied Research Association (TAIRO)
Baroda, Gujarat

Training courses can sometimes be organized at khadi centres by KVIC, Bombay, or directly at the Ghandi Ashram, KG Prayog Samsti, Ahmedabad 380027, Gujarat. Tel. 460524

Other useful sources of information

United Kingdom

The Textile Institute, 10 Blackfriars Street, Manchester M3 5DR
Tel. 061 843 8457. Telex 668297

The Crafts Council, 1 Oxendon Street, London SW1Y 4AT. Tel. 071 930 4811

Society of Dyers and Colourists, PO Box 244, Perkin House, 82 Grattan Road, Bradford, W. Yorks BD1 2JB

Association of Guilds of Weavers Spinners and Dyers, BCM 963 London, WC1N 3XX

India

Khadi and Village Industries Commission, Irla, Vile Parle, Bombay 400056

Centre for Appropriate Technology, Indian Institute of Technology, Hauz Khas, New Delhi. 110016

Rajasthan Small Industries Corp. (RAJSICO)
2nd Floor, Udyog Bhawan, Tilak Marg, Jaipur, 302005

Aga Khan Rural Support Programme, Choice Premises, Swastik Crossroads, Navrangpura, Ahmedabad 380009, Gujarat.

Published sources of information

Society of Dyers and Colourists, Colour Index (This is the only comparative source of information on all known natural and manufactured dyes. It includes the chemical constitution of the dye and manufacturers' trade names. It is extremely expensive.)

Canning, A. J., and Jarman, C. G., *Dyeing of Sisal and other Plant Fibres* (Tropical Development and Research Institute, London)

C. H. Giles, *A Laboratory Course in Dyeing* (The Society of Dyers and Colourists, Bradford)

W. Clarke, *An Introduction to Textile Printing* (Newnes-Butterworth)

D. E. R. Trotman, *Dyeing and Chemical Technology of Textile Fibres* (Charles Griffin, London)

Sayyada R. Ghusnavi, *Natural Dyes of Bangladesh* (Vegetable Dye Society, PO Box 268, Dhaka, Bangladesh)

Zumbuhl, Hugo, *Tintes Naturales* (Brasilia 200, San Carlos, Hyo, Peru) (in Spanish)

Fernandes, Betsabe, and Cajias, Martha, *Manual de Tintes Naturales* (Semta, La Paz, Bolivia) (in Spanish)

Plants and Gardens, *Natural Plant Dyeing* (Brooklyn Botanic Garden, Brooklyn, NY 11225)

Dalby, G, *Natural Dyes — Fast or Fugitive* (Ashill Publications, Dulverton, Somerset, England)

Ilse Noy, *Dyeing with Plants in Zimbabwe* (ZIMFEP, Harara, Zimbabwe)

Books and papers containing more specialized information on dyeing and printing.

Gram Praudyogiki, vol. 2, no. 3, Sept. 1981. 'Textile printing for rural artisans' (Centre for Rural Development and Appropriate Technology, Indian Institute of Technology Hauz Khaz, N. Delhi 110016)

Books on testing

Standard methods for the determination of the colour fastness of textiles (Society of Dyers and Colourists)

British Standards Institution, *Methods of test for colour fastness of textiles and leather,* BS 1006 (BSI London)

APPENDIX 1

SOME TECHNICAL TERMS USED IN DYEING

Dye manufacturers' pattern cards and technical information sheets sometimes contain terms with which small-scale producers may not be familiar or which may be confused with similar terms used in a different situation. A few examples follow.

The **DYEBATH** refers to the water containing the dye and chemicals, sometimes called the **DYELIQUOR**. The container for the dyebath is sometimes called the **DYE VESSEL**, or simply the **DYEING MACHINE**.

The material to be dyed is usually **WET-OUT** in the dyebath before dyeing by immersion in water and a detergent. The dyebath is then **SET** with all the chemicals and dyes necessary to carry out the dyeing.

The process of transfer of the dye from the dyebath to the fibre being dyed is called the **EXHAUSTION** of the dyebath and is usually expressed as a percentage: e.g., 80% **EXHAUSTION** would mean that 80% of the original dye had dyed the fibre and 20% is left in the dyebath. The amount of dye on the fibre when dyeing has been completed determines the **DEPTH** of the dyeing.

The dyebath is **LOADED** with the material to be dyed and sometimes the dyebath is **DROPPED**, that is, run to waste without gradual dilution with fresh water, which would normally be the case.

During and after dyeing it is important that the material being dyed is **LEVEL**, that is, that the depth of shade is the same throughout all the material being dyed and that the material is evenly **PENETRATED**, that is, that the yarn or fabric does not appear lighter if the material is untwisted or cut. **UNLEVEL** dyeings can be avoided by careful dyeing, by adding the dye and chemical **DYEING ASSISTANTS** to the dyebath carefully, by removal of the material from the dyebath while this is taking place, and by careful movement of the material in the dyebath during dyeing, sometimes called **WORKING**. The **RATE OF DYEING** must be controlled, that is, the rate at which the dye is taken up by the fibre, by control of the rate at which the temperature of the dyebath is raised or the dyeing assistants are added. The dye must not **STRIKE** too quickly, and sufficient time must be allowed for the dye to **MIGRATE**, that is, transfer from heavily dyed to lightly dyed parts of the material.

Once dyeing is complete a small sample or **SWATCH** may be removed, washed, and dried to compare with a **PATTERN** or to keep as a record. If the dyeing is not the same **SHADE** as the pattern **(OFF-SHADE)**, it may be necessary to add more dyes to the dyebath (these would be called **SHADING** dyes) until the swatch and the pattern appear the same **(ON-SHADE)** or a **MATCH**.

If a dyeing is faulty in some respect or not the correct shade it can sometimes be **STRIPPED**, that is, given a treatment to remove the dye completely or partly, so that the material can be re-dyed.

All materials need to be washed after dyeing or printing to remove loose dye and dyeing assistants or printing thickeners. When this washing process includes a detergent or soap it will be called **SOAPING-OFF**.

Many terms are used to compare the appearance of two coloured materials. One material may differ from another in **HUE** — it is redder, yellower, bluer, etc. — and it will also be compared in **DEPTH**, that is, it may contain less dye than another in which case it may be called weaker or paler or thinner. One material may also be **DULLER** or **BRIGHTER** than another. For all practical purposes the dyer can only control the hue and dullness or brightness, which he usually combines to describe the **SHADE** of dyeing, and the **DEPTH OF SHADE**, that is the amount of dye which is necessary to **MATCH** the pattern.

APPENDIX 2

PREPARATION AND AFTERTREATMENT OF YARN AND FABRIC

Thorough and even preparation of yarn and fabric before dyeing and printing and thorough washing after dyeing and printing should be an essential part of the colouration process.

Most yarns and fabrics will contain many impurities which must be removed by scouring if the material is to be dyed and printed, or the dyeing will be uneven and will have reduced fastness, particularly to rubbing and wet treatments. In the case of yarn or fabric dyed or printed with vat, azoic, or sulphur dyes, it is particularly important that the dyed or printed material is aftertreated with soap or detergent solution at as high a temperature as possible, to remove loose particles of dye and improve the rubbing and light fastness; there is also a considerable change of shade.

These processes have a relatively high cost in energy terms, indeed the preparation and aftertreatment may cost more than the dyeing, but should nevertheless be regarded as essential. Most of the treatments given have been modified to take account of some inefficiency in processing such as a reduced scouring temperature. The treatments are also based upon the use of a detergent, Lissapol N (ICI), which is widely available, although of course any similar non-ionic product would be suitable.

METHODS

(a) Preparation of cotton for dyeing or printing
Boil the yarn or fabric (or treat at as high a temperature as possible) in a solution containing 2 gm/l Lissapol N and 2 - 5 gm/l sodium carbonate for 30 minutes and then remove and wash thoroughly in cold water. For very seedy or dirty yarn or fabric it may be necessary to repeat this treatment. The scouring process should not be prolonged unduly, or dirt and wax may be re-deposited on the material. Two short scours are much better than one long one, although soaking the material overnight in warm water before scouring may be an advantage.

This should be regarded as the minimum pretreatment for cotton.

(b) Preparation of silk fabric for printing
The fabric should be scoured gently in a solution containing 2 gm/l Lissapol N at 40°C for 30 minutes followed by washing in cold water.

(c) Preparation of wool for dyeing or printing
The yarn or fabric is scoured in a solution containing 2 gm/l Lissapol N at 40°C for 20 minutes followed by washing in cold water. If the wool is very dirty it should be given two treatments, the first in a solution containing 2 gm/l Lissapol N and 2 gm/l sodium bicarbonate at 40°C for 20 minutes followed by a second treatment using only Lissapol N and then washing in cold water. The material should be handled as gently as possible to prevent felting.

(d) Degumming silk
The following treatment is designed to remove completely the silk gum.

1   Soak the silk for one hour at 50°C in a solution containing 2 gm/l sodium carbonate. Allow to cool overnight in this solution.

2   Treat the silk for 2-3 hours at 90-95°C in a solution containing 10 gm/l soft soap and 0.5 gm/l sodium carbonate. (This may be repeated with a fresh solution.)

3   Treat for 5 minutes at 50°C in a solution containing 1 gm/l sodium carbonate.

4   Wash the silk in clean warm water and then cold water.

Bleaching is the removal of some or all of the natural colour in fibres. It is generally only used when a yarn or fabric must be dyed to a very pale, bright colour. Where the fibre has a strong natural colour, such as in heavily pigmented hair fibres or wild silk, it is very difficult to bring about anything more than a slight change of colour by bleaching, without the danger of damaging the fibre by the treatment.

(e) Bleaching cotton or linen
The clean scoured material is treated at 20°C in a solution containing 2 gm/l sodium carbonate for 15 minutes. (The pH of the solution should be 9.) Then add 10 ml of sodium hypochlorite solution/litre of bleaching bath and treat for 2-4 hours at 20°C. (The hypochlorite solution should contain 35 gm available chlorine per litre.) Finally wash the material very thoroughly in cold water.

It is important that when bleaching with hypochlorite solutions clean, soft water is used, not contaminated with iron or copper, and that stainless steel, wood, ceramic, or concrete bleaching tubs should be used which are protected from strong sunlight.

(f) Bleaching wool
The clean scoured material is treated at 50°C in a solution containing 3 gm/l sodium pyrophosphate and 10 ml/l hydrogen peroxide (35% sol) for 2 hours. The wool is left to cool in this solution overnight or until white, and then washed very thoroughly in cold water.

(g) Bleaching silk
The degummed silk is treated at 70°C in a solution containing 3 gm/l sodium pyrophosphate and 13 ml/l hydrogen peroxide (35% sol) for 2 hours followed by washing very thoroughly in cold water.

When bleaching with hydrogen peroxide solutions it is important that clean, soft water is used, not contaminated with iron or copper, and that stainless steel, wood, ceramic, or concrete bleaching tubs are used, which are out of strong sunlight and do not have brass or copper taps or drains.

(h) Aftertreatment of yarn or fabric dyed or printed with reactive dyes
The material is washed in a solution containing 1 gm/l Lissapol N at as high a temperature as possible for 20 minutes, followed by washing in cold water. For very dark colours, particularly reds, it may be necessary to repeat this process until the dyeing or print does not bleed during drying. The wet fastness of reactive dyes is very good; they must, however, be thoroughly washed after dyeing or printing. If the coloured materials are dyed or printed a deep shade, particularly one containing red, and are to be stored in hot and humid conditions, there is some advantage to be gained by aftertreating the material

with a dye-fixing agent. There are many such products available, Matexil FC-PN (ICI) being typical. Their use does, however, cause some small change of colour and some loss of light fastness, and they should not therefore be used on pale shades. It must be stressed that they are not a substitute for thorough washing after dyeing.

Matexil FC-PN should be added to the final washing-off bath: an amount equal to half the weight of dye used should be pasted with cold water and added to the final wash at 20°C. Treat the material in this solution for 20 minutes and then remove and dry without rinsing.

(i) Aftertreatment of yarn or fabric dyed or printed with vat or azoic dyes
The material is boiled in a solution containing 2 gm/l soft green soap or Lissapol N for 15 minutes, followed by hot and cold washing in water.

APPENDIX 3

DYEING WOOL WITH ACID AND METAL COMPLEX DYES

Before dyeing the wool must be thoroughly prepared by scouring as described in Appendix 2.

REAGENTS NEEDED
Range of suitable acid dyes (equalizing, milling, or super milling)
Range of suitable pre-metallized dyes (2:1 metal complex and chrome)
Glauber's salt (sodium sulphate crystals)
Acetic acid (30% solution)
Sulphuric acid (85% solution) or formic acid (96% solution)
Ammonium sulphate or acetate

DYEING METHOD

(a) Equalizing acid dyes
Wet out the material to be dyed in a dyebath at 50°C containing 3-4% sulphuric acid or 4% formic acid and 10% Glauber's salt, all quantities based on the weight of material being dyed. (The dyebath should have a pH value of 2-3.) After 5 minutes add the necessary quantity of well-dissolved dye and then gradually raise the temperature over a period of 30 minutes to 95-100°C and continue dyeing at this temperature for 30-40 minutes.

(b) Milling acid dyes
Wet-out the material to be dyed in a dyebath at 40°C containing 1-3% acetic acid and 5% Glauber's salt crystals, all based on the weight of material being dyed. (The dyebath should have a pH value of 4.) After 5 minutes add the necessary quantity of well-dissolved dye and then gradually raise the temperature over a period of 30 minutes to 95°C and continue dyeing at this temperature for 30-40 minutes.

(c) Super milling and 2:1 pre-metallized dyes
Wet-out the material to be dyed in a dyebath at 30°C containing 2-5% ammonium sulphate or acetate, based on the weight of material being dyed. (The dyebath should have a pH value of 6-7.) After 5 minutes add the necessary quantity of well-dissolved dye and then gradually raise the temperature over a period of 30 minutes to 95°C and continue dyeing at this temperature for 30-40 minutes.

In all cases, after dyeing is completed the material should be washed very thoroughly in clean cold water and then dried.

It is always best during dyeing to remove the material being dyed from the dyebath whilst the dissolved dye is being added, if this is possible.

APPENDIX 4

DYEING COTTON, VISCOSE RAYON, OR LINEN WITH DIRECT DYES

Before dyeing the yarn or fabric must be thoroughly prepared for dyeing by scouring as described in Appendix 2.

REAGENTS NEEDED
Range of direct dyes. (If possible the Society of Dyers and Colourists classification should be known, see Chapter 2.)

Glauber's salt (sodium sulphate crystals)
Common salt (sodium chloride)
Lissapol N (ICI)
Matexil FC-PN (ICI)

DYEING METHOD
Wet-out the material to be dyed in a dyebath at 30°C containing 0.5 ml/l Lissapol N. After 5 minutes add the necessary quantity of pre-dissolved dye and then gradually raise the temperature of the dyebath to 85-90°C over a period of 30 minutes and continue to dye at that temperature for 45 minutes. From 5 to 20% common salt or Glauber's salt can be added according to the depth of shade to increase the exhaustion of the dye and this should be added slowly or quickly during dyeing according to the dye classification. Finally wash thoroughly in cold water.

NOTES
(a) It is always best to remove the material being dyed from the dyebath whilst the dye is being added.

(b) Where the dyeing classification is not known, it is safest to add the necessary quantity of salt in small portions to the dyebath as the temperature is being slowly raised. Where the dyeing must have moderately good wet fastness, it can be aftertreated with Matexil FC-PN in a similar manner to the aftertreatment of some reactive dyes as described in Appendix 2 (h). For direct dyes the temperature of the treatment should, however, be raised to 50°C and the cotton washed in cold water afterwards.

(c) Where the dyeing classification is known it is not advisable to mix dyes from group A with those from group C.

APPENDIX 5

DYEING COTTON, VISCOSE RAYON, OR LINEN WITH REACTIVE DYES (PROCION MX)

Before dyeing the yarn or fabric must be thoroughly prepared by scouring as described in Appendix 2.

REAGENTS NEEDED
Range of reactive dyes (Procion MX type)
Sodium chloride
Sodium carbonate
Acetic acid (30% solution)
Matexil FC-PN (ICI)

DYEING METHOD
Wet-out the material to be dyed in a dyebath at 30°C and adjust the pH to 6-7 with acetic acid (check with test papers). Make sure all the material is at the same pH. Lift the yarn from the dyebath and add the necessary quantity of dye dissolved in some water from the bath (not hot water). Mix thoroughly, add the yarn and turn on the dyesticks for 5 minutes. Add a quarter of the sodium chloride and dye for 10 minutes; repeat until all the salt has been added.

Make up a solution containing the necessary quantity of sodium carbonate and divide into six lots with at least two very small lots, e.g. for 1000ml divide into 50, 50, 100, 200, 200, 400ml.

Lift the yarn and add 50ml sodium carbonate sol., add the yarn and turn vigorously on the sticks for 10 minutes. Repeat until all the sodium carbonate solution has been added. Dye for a further 20 minutes. Remove the material and wash in cold water. Then wash the material in a solution containing 1gm/l Lissapol N at 80°C for 20 minutes followed by cold washing. If necessary aftertreat the material with Matexil FC-PN by the method in Appendix 2.

QUANTITIES OF REAGENTS

Amount of dye (% dye on the weight of yarn)	Sodium chloride (gm/litre of dyebath)	Sodium carbonate (gm/litre of dyebath)
Up to 0.5%	20gm/1	3gm/1
0.5% to 2.0%	25gm/1	4gm/1
2.0% to 4.0%	35gm/1	8gm/1
Above 4.0%	45gm/1	10gm/1

NOTES
(a) Always add the sodium carbonate solution very slowly at first: most uneven dyeing occurs because this is added too quickly.

(b) Hot washing is very important if good wet fastness is to be achieved.

APPENDIX 6

DYEING SILK WITH ACID, METAL COMPLEX, AND REACTIVE DYES

Before dyeing the silk must be thoroughly prepared by scouring and degumming by the method described in Appendix 2 (d).

Reagents needed
Range of milling and super milling acid dyes, 2:1 metal complex and reactive dyes.

Glauber's salt (sodium sulphate crystals)
Acetic acid (30% solution)
Ammonium sulphate
Soda ash (sodium carbonate)
Unisol BTI (ICI) (If this product is not available some of the scouring solution left after degumming can be used.)
Lissapol N (ICI)

DYEING METHOD

(a) Acid and 2:1 metal complex dyes
Wet-out the material to be dyed in a dyebath at 30°C containing 2% ammonium sulphate and 2% Unisol BT, all quantities based on the weight of material being dyed. After 5 minutes add the necessary quantity of pre-dissolved dye and then gradually over a period of 30 minutes raise the temperature to 85°C and continue dyeing at this temperature for 30-40 minutes. (If the dye used does not exhaust very well the dyebath should be cooled to 50°C and 3-4% acetic acid added, followed by raising the temperature gradually back to 85°C.)

(b) REACTIVE DYES (Procion MX type, ICI)
Wet-out the material to be dyed in a dyebath at 30°C containing the necessary amount of pre-dissolved dye, for 15 minutes then add 5-20 grams/litre Glauber's salt and dye for 15 minutes. Add a further 5-20 grams/litre and dye for 15 minutes then gradually raise the temperature of the dyebath over a period of 30 minutes to 50°C. Dye at this temperature for 15 minutes and then slowly add 2 grams/litre pre-dissolved soda ash and continue dyeing for 30-40 minutes. After dyeing wash the material thoroughly in cold water containing 0.5 grams/litre soda ash and then scour in a solution containing 0.2 grams/litre detergent, such as Lissapol N (ICI) at 60-70°C for 10 minutes followed by washing in cold water.

For dyeing method (a) the material should be washed very thoroughly in cold water after dyeing, then dried.

In all cases it is best during dyeing to remove the material being dyed from the dyebath whilst the dissolved dye is being added, if this is possible.

APPENDIX 7

PRINTING WOOL AND SILK WITH REACTIVE DYES (PROCION MX) WITHOUT STEAMING

Before printing, the fabrics should be thoroughly prepared by washing in a solution containing Lissapol N at a low temperature (see Appendix 2).

REAGENTS NEEDED
Range of Procion MX dyes
Urea
Sodium alginate thickening (Manutex RS) (This is best made up as a stock thickening by dissolving 40 gm Manutex in every 1000 ml water. Mix with a high-speed stirrer and leave overnight.)
Sodium metabisulphite
Acetic acid (30% solution)

PRINTING METHOD
The quantities of reagents given are intended to make 1000 gm printing paste.

Make up the paste by dissolving 300 gm urea in 280 ml water. Some heat will be required to make the urea dissolve completely.

Cool the solution and add 20 gm sodium metabisulphite, stir to dissolve. Add this solution to 400 gm sodium alginate thickening and stir well. Add just sufficient acetic acid to bring the pH to 5, stir well.

To make this paste thinner add a little more water, and thicken by adding less water. This mixture forms the basic printing paste and will keep for several days in a sealed container.

Immediately before printing add the necessary amount of Procion dye, as a dry powder or made into a paste with a little cold water. Mix the dye into the paste very thoroughly.

Once the dye has been added to the paste it must be used as quickly as possible, certainly within one working day and more quickly in a hot climate.

During printing the printed mark must not be allowed to dry out completely. This can be achieved by covering the printing table with a polythene sheet and fixing the fabric to be printed to this. If a length of fabric is being printed the printed sections should also be covered with polythene until the whole length is completed, taking care not to 'mark-off' on the printed fabric as the polythene is moved.

When printing is complete the whole length of fabric is covered with polythene and rolled up so that the fabric is between layers of polythene. The roll is stored overnight and then the fabric is washed. The polythene can be washed, dried, and used again. The printed fabric should first be soaked for a few minutes in cold water containing a litle ammonia solution, followed by hot and cold washing. For printed silk, the fabric may then be aftertreated with Matexil FC-PN as described in Appendix 2(h).

NOTES
(a) Although this is a very successful method for printing wool and silk where expensive equipment such as a steamer is not available, care and practice are needed to make the process work easily. It is very important to maintain the

proportion of urea and bisulphite in each 1000 gm paste, so that if a reduction is made (to print a paler colour), the reduction must be made with the made-up thickening, not with water.

(b) Because the fabric is stored for a long period when the printing is still damp, closely fitted designs, particularly where different printed marks may overlap slightly, are liable to bleed from one colour into the adjacent one, during storage. This means that such designs must be printed by a two-stage process, washing and drying the fabric between prints. This is usually successful in block-printing, but cannot be used in screen printing.

(c) The process can be used also for producing patterned yarns, the yarn hank or warp being painted with different colours or patterns and then stored in a polythene bag overnight before washing.

(d) The process is suitable for almost all groups of reactive dyes, including Procion MX and H, Cibacron pront, Levafix E, Drimarene R, Reactofil, Drimalan F, Verofix, but not Remazol or Lanasol.

APPENDIX 8

PRINTING COTTON FABRICS WITH REACTIVE DYES (PROCION MX) (WITH OR WITHOUT STEAMING)

Before printing, fabrics must be thoroughly and evenly prepared by scouring in a solution containing sodium carbonate and Lissapol N (see Appendix 2). If very bright colours are to be printed the fabric should also be bleached, and best results are obtained by printing fabrics made from mercerized and bleached yarn.

REAGENTS NEEDED
Procion MX dyes
Urea
Sodium alginate thickening (Manutex RS)   (This is best made up as a 4% stock solution by dissolving 40 gm Manutex in every 1000 ml water. Mix with a stirrer and leave overnight until a smooth paste is formed.)

Sodium bicarbonate
Sodium carbonate

PRINTING METHOD
The quantities of reagents given are intended to make 1000 gms of printing paste.

Make up the paste by dissolving 30 gm urea in 100 ml water. Add to this solution 20 gm sodium bicarbonate and 2 gm sodium carbonate and stir until dissolved or mixed very thoroughly. Add this mixture to 700 gm of the 4% Manutex stock solution and mix very thoroughly until a smooth paste is formed. It is important that the solution of urea, sodium bicarbonate, and sodium carbonate is evenly mixed with the thickening. To make the printing paste thinner use a little more water; to make it thicker use less water. This mixture forms the basic printing paste and will keep for several days in a sealed container.

Immediately before printing add the necessary amount of Procion dye. This may be added as a dry powder or made into a paste with a little cold water. Mix the dye into the paste very thoroughly.

Once the dye has been added to the printing paste it must be used as quickly as possible, certainly within one working day and more quickly than this in a very hot climate.

After printing, allow the fabric to dry on the printing table and then remove and hang in a warm, humid atmosphere for several hours or preferably overnight. High temperatures and high humidity give good dye fixation; if the atmosphere is too dry poor fixation will be achieved. Finally wash the printed fabric in cold water until all loose dye and thickening have been removed, then wash the fabric in very hot water containing 2gm/l Lissapol N. Repeat if necessary. Finally wash again in cold water. If very dark colours tend to bleed during drying the washing has not been sufficiently severe. Dark colours can also be aftertreated with Matexil FC-PN (see Appendix 2).

NOTES
(a) If a reliable steamer is available, the same printing recipe can be used but sodium carbonate should not be added to the printing paste. After printing

dry the fabric and steam for 10 minutes at atmospheric pressure followed by washing as before.

(b) The printing pastes containing dye can be mixed in any proportions, but to make a reduction in strength (to print a paler colour) do not add water. Always add more of the basic printing paste so that the concentration of reagents is maintained.

(c) If the atmosphere is very dry and a steamer is not available, suitable conditions for dye fixation can be achieved by hanging the printed fabrics in a warm room in which the floor is kept constantly wet and containers of water are left around.

APPENDIX 9

PRINTING COTTON FABRICS WITH PIGMENTS

Before printing, the fabrics must be thoroughly and evenly prepared by scouring in a solution containing sodium carbonate and Lissapol N (see Appendix 2). If very bright colours are to be printed the fabric should also be bleached.

REAGENTS NEEDED

Range of pigment colours (From any manufacturer but see Note (a).)
Pigment binder, e.g. Acramin SLN 130% (Bayer)
Emulsifier, e.g. Emulsifier L(Bayer)
Sodium alginate thickening (Manutex RS.) This is best made up as a 4% stock solution by dissolving 40 gm Manutex in every 1000 gm water. Mix with a stirrer and leave overnight until a smooth paste is formed.)

Diammonium phosphate sol. This is best made up as a stock solution by dissolving 50 gm diammonium phosphate in every 100 gm water.)

Cross-linking agent, e.g. Acrafix M(Bayer)
White spirit

PRINTING METHOD

The quantities of reagents given are intended to make 1000 gm printing paste.

Make up the printing paste by mixing together by means of a high-speed stirrer 100 gm of the 4% sodium alginate thickening, 20 gm of the Emulsifier L and 300 gm of Acramin SLN 130%. Add 10 gm Acrafix M and then slowly add 700 gm white spirit, stirring constantly while the white spirit is added. Stir for about three minutes, when the paste should have the consistency of very thick cream. This forms the basic printing paste and will keep in a sealed container for several days. To control the thickness of the paste add more white spirit to make the paste thicker and less to make it thinner.

Immediately before printing add the necessary amount of colour pigment and 20 gm of the diammonium phosphate solution and stir thoroughly by hand. This printing paste should be used the same day if the climate is hot.

After printing the fabric should be allowed to dry on the printing table and then, if a high-temperature baker is available, heated for 4 - 5 minutes at 150°C. If hot air baking is not available, the fabric can be dried in the sun for several days followed by steaming and washing, or simply dried in the sun. The printing recipe given has been slightly modified to make some allowances for poor fixation conditions and the fabrics do not normally need to be washed after printing, but the softness is usually improved by washing, after drying for about one week.

NOTES

(a) Before printing the fabric must be dry and in a neutral condition (not alkaline) if good fixation is to be obtained.

(b) A large amount of binder has been included in the recipe to allow for poor fixation conditions, but if fixation conditions are good, i.e. a baker is available, the amount of binder can be reduced to about 200 gm per kg of printing paste.

(c) It is very important always to use good quality reagents of known strength. If the binder or pigments have been watered down to reduce cost, it will be impossible to obtain the correct viscosity of printing paste and therefore to obtain good quality prints.

APPENDIX 10

EFFLUENT DISPOSAL

GENERAL SITUATION

The building of a centrally located dyehouse of the type described in Chapter 5, in which it is intended to dye both yarns and fabrics as well as carrying out some scouring and washing of printed fabrics, is likely to cause some problems of effluent disposal. It is understood that these problems could be purely local in the sense that there may be no known national regulations about these matters, but at the very least efficient disposal should be regarded as a matter of good housekeeping and a good example to others.

The most obvious effect of centralization will be caused by the use of reactive dyes, which always cause effluent to be highly coloured and therefore very visible when discharged into a waterway or pond. The toxicity of the effluent created by dyeing is not likely to be a problem, from the point of view of either quantity or nature. The use of reactive dye printing will create similar problems, since fabrics must be hot washed after printing, unlike pigment-printed fabrics which in general do not make an effluent disposal problem.

QUANTITIES OF EFFLUENT

Since a common drainage system is being suggested, it will not be practicable to separate effluent produced during washing and scouring from that produced during dyeing. The total quantity from the proposed dyehouse is therefore likely to be of the order of 2000 gallons for an 8-hour working day, much of it highly coloured.

TYPE OF EFFLUENT

(a) from scouring: containing organic matter removed from cotton and detergent and alkali residues.

(b) from bleaching: containing mostly residues of alkalis and bleaching agents. Although it may not be intended to carry out bleaching in the new dyehouse, but in concrete tubs or tanks located close to the dyehouse, the bleaching effluent could with some advantage be added to that from dyeing for disposal if this could be easily arranged.

(c) from dyeing: containing dye residues and some alkali and common salt. Occasionally some residues from the use of stripping agents, such as sodium hydrosulphite, but only in relatively small quantities.

(d) from printing: containing printing paste residues, thickening agents, and substantial amounts of dye or pigment from unused printing paste. Also some detergent and dye removed during fabric washing after printing.

TREATMENT

In an ideal situation the effluent, after treatment, should be colourless and neutral, ready to dilute into a large volume of water such as a water system without causing any problems. This would be possible to achieve, although it would take time and trouble to do so and would represent an additional cost per unit of material dyed or printed in terms of both increased overheads and increased running costs. For the relatively small amount of effluent produced, and in the absence of any regulations requiring treatment, there must be a temptation to run the untreated waste directly into the nearest water course or pond. It is possible therefore to specify a range of treatments, from no treatment at all to a moderate treatment which, in particular circumstances, will give a satisfactory effluent.

(a) If the effluent can be run directly into a moderately large pond, which can be used solely for the purpose of storing and diluting it and which will not cause any local problems with drainage into ground water, this is probably the cheapest solution. The effluent should be run into the pond with as much aeration as possible, when a combination of sedimentation and biological action will take place over a period of time, particularly in the presence of strong sunlight. This will cause a desposit of sludge to form which may eventually cause fermentation problems in hot weather, but this is not likely to happen for a long time unless the pond is too small.

(b) If the effluent is to be treated before being released into, say, a waterway, some form of settling and storage tank must be used. In the tank it can be neutralized and the colour removed or diminished by flocculation and coagulation. This is achieved by the addition of a chemical agent which forms a blanket of flocculant material with the dye in the effluent, which then settles to form a sludge leaving the remaining liquid relatively clear. This can be best achieved by dividing the tank so that half can be treated and settled when full while the other half is filling. This treatment will give a relatively clear effluent, but of course it will still contain quantities of dissolved salts such as sodium carbonate, sodium chloride, acids, etc., and there is no economic way to remove these.

The amount of flocculating agent used depends upon the composition of the effluent and must be determined by experimentation. The most commonly used agent is potassium aluminium sulphate (alum) and is used in quantities up to 500 mg per litre of effluent. It is also possible to use a wide range of proprietary products as flocculating aids such as Welgum S (Alginate Industries), but many of these may not be readily available.

The effluent produced is likely to be alkaline, because of the dyeing process and method of scouring. Ideally this should be neutralized by the addition of a small amount of acid before flocculation, but tests should be undertaken to see if flocculation is effective with the untreated effluent.

METHOD

The illustration shows a tank which would be suitable, if it is decided to use one. The tank has two chambers with a total storage capacity of 24,000 gallons which should allow one week's effluent to be stored and treated at a time. Dimensions have not been included, since it will be necessary to arrange these so that a natural fall is allowed to drain the tank, unless a pump is to be used. If the tank is wholly below ground level this will of course be the only method of emptying. Once one side is full the effluent is neutralized (if necessary) and then the flocculating agent is added in solution and stirred until flocculation is complete.

The flocs may settle fairly quickly, but sometimes may require precipitation by addition of acid or lime which forms a sludge on the bottom of the tank. The clear liquid can then be run to waste and the tank refilled with effluent.

The sludge must be removed occasionally by digging out and disposed of in a suitable manner. It must be stressed that at all times the process will require careful control to be effective and is therefore likely to be time-consuming and moderately expensive to operate.

(not to scale)

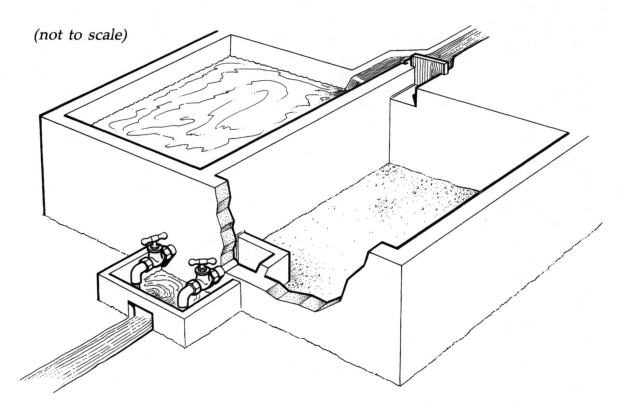

Illustration 15 Small-scale settling tank for effluent

www.ingramcontent.com/pod-product-compliance
Lightning Source LLC
Jackson TN
JSHW052138131224
75386JS00039B/1298